TRAINING FOR WAR GAMES
One Man's National Service

TRAINING
FOR WAR GAMES

One Man's National Service

Len Woodrup

249591

The Book Guild Ltd.
Sussex, England

The Book Guild Ltd.,
25 High Street,
Lewes, Sussex

First published 1993
© Len Woodrup 1993
Set in Baskerville
Typesetting by Kudos Graphics
Slinfold, Horsham, West Sussex

Printed in Great Britain by
Antony Rowe Ltd.,
Chippenham, Wiltshire.

A catalogue record for this book is
available from the British Library

ISBN 0 86332 862 5

CONTENTS

1

Introduction to Conscription

Today, the three armed services – the Royal Navy, the Army and the Royal Air Force – rely on volunteers to provide the manpower for all the tasks which the Ministry of Defence considers to be necessary for the defence of the realm. In the First World War conscription was introduced in 1916, to provide replacements for the thousands of British troops killed or wounded in Europe.

Conscription was used again for the Second World War. A bill was put before Parliament in April 1939, it became statute in May and the first conscripts were called up in July, two months before the war broke out.

The men who were called up for military service were informed it was for the duration of the emergency, ie the war, but conscription continued into the 1960s when it was suspended.

Post war National Service meant that all men aged eighteen or over were liable to be called up to serve King and Country, unless they were medically unfit or in a reserved occupation. Individuals taking graduate/post-graduate studies, professional training or trade training courses could apply for, and usually obtained, deferred call-up. If a person managed to be deferred until he was twenty-six, he was no longer liable to conscription, but such lucky persons were rare. Very few escaped the net.

National Service in the Royal Air Force was as follows. You were:

1. Directed to have a medical examination at a nearby city medical unit.

2. Directed to attend a reception unit or called up. The stay here usually lasted for one week and you were kitted out, had a trade test, trade selection or aircrew interview. Some lucky individuals were declared unfit following medical examinations and were discharged.

3. Posted to a basic training camp for eight weeks to acquire the art of the immediate response to commands and instructions, and perfecting the drill movements associated with the commands. This period was generally referred to as 'square bashing '.

4. Posted to a training school – flying, radar and radio, instrument, catering, nursing and so on. A posting to the electrical school was for twenty-two weeks.

5. Posted to an operational unit, this was generally a permanent posting for the remaining service period.

Annual leave was fourteen days per year and several travel warrants were available each year. Other leave was given in the form of thirty-six, forty-eight and seventy-two hour passes – commonly referred to as weekend passes. When I was on a permanent posting I took my leave by a series of consequent passes – a seventy-two hour pass for Saturday, Sunday and

Monday, then a pass for four days annual leave, Tuesday, Wednesday, Thursday and Friday: and finally a forty-eight hour pass for Saturday and Sunday. That resulted in eight days leave but ten day annual still left. Sometimes it was possible to get two seventy-two hour passes and only take three days annual leave.

At the time of my call up a National Service airman's weekly pay was twenty-eight shillings (£1.40), some airmen elected to make an allowance of seven shillings (35p) to their nearest next of kin. This left only twenty-one shillings (£1.05) and any savings to pay for soap, boot polish, metal polish, blanco, barrack damages as well as beer, cigarettes, char and wads (tea and sandwiches), and generally keeping one in the manner to which one had been accustomed to before call up.

Also at that time a regular AC1 was paid two pounds, fourteen shillings (£2.60p) per week. Nearly twice that of a National serviceman for exactly the same work.

One had to be aware of what was contained in KRs (King's Regulations – later Queen's Regulations) and SSOs (Station Standing Orders) so that one tried to ensure that no officer or NCO or snoop could pin a charge on your for ignoring some part of the regulations or orders.

Today, advocates of the short sharp shock treatment for delinquents suggest the government should re-introduce National Service to instil some discipline into the youth of today. The majority of National Servicemen were not delinquents and they were serving King and Country and later Queen and Country, and many of them died defending the peace. They served their country, not a custodial sentence.

9

2

Royal Air Force Ranks and Command Structure

Before moving on to basic training I think a description of ranks and command structure would help you to understand the conscripts' position in the Royal Air Force pecking order – his title and rank was AC2 or Aircraftman 2, the lowest of the low and at any higher ranker's beck and call. Starting with lowest of the low, there were

Aircraftmen:

Aircraftman (1 or 2)	– AC plonk, and sprog or erk,
Leading Aircraftman	– LAC,
Senior Aircraftmen	– SAC,
Junior Technician	– JT.

Non Commissioned Officers – NCOs:

Corporal,
Corporal Technician,
Sergeant,
Sergeant Technician,
Flight Sergeant –   Known as Chief or chiefy when he was a respected section leader, most were.

Chief Technician,
Warrant Officer –   When this rank carried the
                     title of Station Warrant
                     Officer – SWO – the holder
                     was God Almighty and
                     worse than any RSM in the
                     army.

Commissioned Officers:

Pilot Officer,
Flying Officer,
Flight Lieutenant,
Squadron Leader,
Wing Commander,
Group Captain,
Air Vice Marshal,
Air Marshal,
Marshal of the Royal Air Force.

The three lowest ranks, aircraftman, leading air-craftman and senior aircraftman usually did not pull rank over each other, they generally combined to foil the idiotic orders which, from time to time, came down from above.

The Command Structure from the top down was:

MINISTRY OF DEFENCE (now)
AIR MINISTRY, (then)

COMMANDS: Training,
          Fighter.
          Bomber.
          Coastal,
          Transport.

11

A COMMAND was divided into GROUPS.

A GROUP was divided into WINGS.

A WING was made up of a number of SQUADRONS.

A SQUADRON was made up of several FLIGHTS.

A FLIGHT was comprised of several SECTIONS.

A SECTION was a collection of individuals working as a team to achieve a common end.

The term applied equally to a section of aircraft pilots or to a craft section responsible for parts of those aircraft or a ground service contributing towards the needs of those aircraft.

3

Call Up

I was called up in September 1951 after nearly four years deferment and was twenty-two years old. The call-up papers directed me to report to the Reception Centre at RAF Padgate, near Warrington, Cheshire.

Included with the call-up papers was a travel warrant from my home town to Warrington Railway Station. It was early afternoon when I arrived at Warrington, from Leeds via Manchester, with about forty other conscripts, all clutching small attaché cases which were the badge of National Servicemen, even when wearing civilian clothes.

The case contained the few items the call-up instructions stated one needed like razor, shaving soap and brush, toothbrush, toothpaste, soap, towels, hair brush and comb, a change of underwear, a pair of pyjamas and – of course – the Bryllcreem.

RAF reception personnel directed us to the RAF transport parked outside the station. The transport was one Bedford three ton troop carrier, a lorry with a canvas canopy covering three rows of wooden benches. After a journey of twenty minutes the truck turned left into RAF Padgate.

The camp initially seemed to be hundreds and hundreds of wooden huts with the odd larger building and water towers scattered here and there. As we were driven through this sea of huts, it could be seen that large open areas of tarmac and concrete also existed within the camp.

The driver stopped the truck on one of these pieces of tarmac, where a sergeant was standing next to one solitary trestle table and one folding chair. The driver climbed down from his cab, he unfastened the locks and lowered the tail board and we jumped down. The NCO had a clip-board under his arm. He told us we were the first of that day's intake. He also arranged us into three ranks and as he walked along each rank he asked each person his name which he checked off against a list on his clipboard.

The Bedford truck came back when he was still halfway along the rear rank. It dropped off another thirty to forty civilians, carrying attaché cases and the checking process continued. The truck came back twice, with more prospective airmen and the checking process was finally completed. The arrival of the last truckload also coincided with several corporals walking onto the square.

We were split into groups of twenty-five and put in the charge of a long time served corporal who tried to march us to the hut which was to be our home for the next week. Once inside the hut we were told to leave our cases on a bed and to fall in outside again. We then marched under the corporal's guidance to the bedding store where we were given four blankets and one pillow case and marched back to the hut once more, only to be told to collect a mug and a knife, fork and spoon from the table in the middle of the room and to fall in outside once again. It was time for tea.

The corporal explained that the mess – dining room – he was about to take us to was the one we would use until posted to a recruit training unit. Tea consisted of

14

baked beans and two sausages, plus tea, bread, butter, jam and a slice of cherry cake. The food was eatable and if it was to continue like this life could become comfortable. But life was not that simple. How can one ruin porridge? Let an RAF cook make it!!

The corporal also showed us the basics of spit and polish or bull and what to purchase for it. He also tried to get us to march as a unit, rather than a disorganised rabble, but he had little success, as we were to find out later when we began Basic Training.

During that first week we were kitted out with the RAF standard issue of uniforms and equipment. We had to have a short back and sides haircut, whether it was needed or not. Everyone had had a medical examination before call-up but yet more examinations and medical tests were made in the week. Some bods had aircrew selection interviews, some had trade tests, while the rest had education tests and aptitude tests to find out who was suitable material for whatever task needed bods at that time.

One day the corporal marched us over to the Education Centre, where we joined about another 200 sprogs, in a large hall. An education officer asked for quiet and told all holders of formal educational qualifications to move out into an adjacent room. I was one of them.

After a while the officer came in and told us we would mark and sort the test papers and aptitude papers which were being taken by the airmen we had left behind. The process went on during the morning and was completed by mid-afternoon. We returned to the main hall and joined the others.

To fill in the rest of the day the officer said we could have general discussion on any topic we wished to choose and he asked for a subject. A red-headed, red-faced, short and rotund airman stood up and proceeded to speak in a very broad Scottish accent, so broad that very few understood what he was saying. The officer asked him to speak more slowly and more precisely and we then heard his suggestion, 'What about home Rule for Scotland?'

The education officer said it was a worthwhile subject and suggested the proposer made his points. The Scottish airman spoke for several unintelligible minutes and at the end the officer asked him:

'What was his name and where was he born?'

The answers were 'Grrrreen Sirrrr – Chesterrrr Sirrrr.' Needless to say that debate ceased and we were dismissed.

Another day the corporal called out about fifteen names and mine was among them. He told us we were going for a trade test. We marched/walked several hundred yards before we were halted outside one of the larger wooden huts.

Inside there was a large central space with plenty of chairs where we sat and waited for our names to be called and then were directed to small cubicles along the sides of the hut. My name and number was called out and I entered the indicated cubicle to find a grey-haired warrant officer at a desk. He asked me to sit down and immediately put both hands out with the thumb and first two fingers of each hand set at right angles to each other and asked if I knew what it represented.

When I had collected myself and put the brain in gear I replied 'Fleming's right hand and left hand rule for generators and motors'.

The next question related to what each finger indicated, then the hands and so on. The test ended with a series of questions on various types of electric motors.

The WO then said I had an X spec, rating, for an electrical fitter/mechanic. I asked him why my choice of radio/radar fitter/mechanic made on one of the many forms filled before call-up was not successful. He replied that since I had been deferred to further a career in electricity I would follow it in the Royal Air Force.

Every airman received his equipment during this week. We were marched to the largest building on the camp, the clothing store, here we were 'kitted out', that is each one of us received the following:

- one greatcoat, with two rows of brass buttons down the front and a half belt at the back, with two buttons.
- one dress uniform – the best blue – a belted tunic jacket with breast pockets, brass buttons and belt with brass buckle, and one pair of trousers and one pair of braces.
- one working uniform – one battle dress jacket and one pair of trousers and another pair of braces.
- two berets and two brass RAF cap badges.
- four light blue shirts, eight collars and two black ties (Collar studs were not provided).
- four vests and four pairs of underpants.
- two pairs of pyjamas.
- two sets of PE vests, shorts, white socks and one pair of plimsols.
- two white hand towels,
- two white bath towels,
- four pairs of airforce blue socks.
- one pair boots and one pair of shoes.
- one housewife and one button stick.

- one large back-pack,
- one small side- ack,
- one webbing belt,
- two webbing shoulder straps,
- one webbing bayonet frog,
- and finally one kitbag to carry it all in.

Additional kit for basic training included:

- one rifle and one rifle sling, drawn from the armoury,
- one tin hat,
- two webbing gaiters,

NOTE – all the webbing equipment had brass fittings which had to be polished and the webbing was covered with blue blanco paste which tended to shine as it was rubbed dry.

The uniforms were not a perfect fit and while tailors made alterations we sprog airmen wore some civilian clothes and those parts of the uniform which fitted. By the end of that first week, when most of our uniforms were complete, we were given sheets of thick brown paper and string to make a parcel of our attaché cases and civilian clothes which were posted home, courtesy of the Royal Air Force.

At the reception unit we had our first experience of fatigues. These were used to fill in any spare days. I was sent with another bod to the Briquette Factory. The factory was a Nissen hut nearly full to the roof with 'nutty slack' (fine coal and coal-dust), tons of it. Other equipment included shovels, cement, a watering can, buckets, wooden seed trays and many small earthenware plant pots. There was also a heap of small grey to black objects which our instructor said were briquettes.

We were told to mix ten parts slack with one part cement and to wet the mixture only so it stuck together. Once mixed it was packed into the plant pots, they were then inverted in the seed trays, the pots removed and the grey to black objects were left to dry. We made several hundred in the day. The next briquette makers would put them onto the finished heap.

In the evenings we practised the art of bull on our kit, and if there was time we would go to either the Red Shield Club or the NAAFI club or just roll into our pits (beds) exhausted from the days activities.

The Red Shield Clubs were run by the Salvation Army. They were quieter and the char and wads were cheaper than at the NAAFI.

At the end of the week we could move around the camp like an organised rabble and were 'fell in' on one of the many parade grounds to be told which recruit training unit we were being posted to. These ranged from West Kirby, near Liverpool, to Bridgenorth in Shropshire, Hornchurch in Essex and Padgate itself.

I was posted to Padgate No 1 Recruit Training Wing. This meant packing one's kit and marching half-a-mile across the station to a group of very basic wooden huts which had some even more basic ablution facilities in huts at the back.

The 'sprog' airman who moved on to basic training generally had a uniform which sagged all over him, a beret which was perched on his head looking like a blue flying saucer, dull boots and all his other possessions jammed in a clean white kit-bag marked with his service number and a pale blue stripe. But after eight weeks of square bashing, rifle drill, PT and the assault course, a smart and extremely fit and airforce-wise aircraftman 2 took his place.

4

Basic Training

Number One Recruit Training Wing at RAF Padgate was comprised of a large parade ground, with a rapidly decaying Lancaster bomber parked across the north east corner. It was only used as a background for flight photographs and to impress parents and visitors at passing out parades. The south east corner contained the drill shed which was only used when the weather was extremely bad. Service roads ran along the north and south sides of the square.

Twenty wooden huts at right angles to the road, fronted the road on the north side and behind these were another twenty huts separated by twelve wash-houses parallel to the road. Beyond the rear line of billets was another service road and over that was the dreaded Number One Wing assault course.

The south side was similarly laid out except there were only thirty billets, in two rows of fifteen. The space opposite the drill shed contained a derelict area which had included a Naafi club, airmens' mess and several billets. The area was being rebuilt.

Facing the west side of the square were four more huts, which contained wing, squadron and flight offices, as well as the Post Office and some NCO's accommodation. A service road ran behind these huts connecting with the others and leading to a security gate allowing access to North Camp which contained the gymnasiums for PT. To the west of the road was a football pitch, the Number Two Wing assault course and a standard WD water tower. The area described above was about 10% of the total area of RAF Padgate.

It was a pleasant late September day when we marched from the Reception Unit side of Padgate to the Recruit Training Wing and the first five wooden huts on the south west side of the square which were to be our homes for the next eight weeks. These huts accommodated more than 100 airmen and five drill instructors (DIs).

My hut was number 123. We became Number One Flight, in A Squadron, in Number One Wing. Padgate had two recruit training wings. Other drill instructors appeared from time to time, but the original five were with us for most of the eight weeks. The majority of us sprogs had been deferred and many had degrees or Higher and Ordinary National Certificates and School Certificates.

During the following weeks the working hours were mainly spent on the parade ground – square bashing, being ordered 'squad attention', 'squad left turn – about turn – quick march – halt – wait for it – by the left quick march – halt – slope arms – order arms – slope arms – present arms – slope arms – right turn – by the left quick march – left wheel – about turn – right wheel – halt – left turn – right dress – eyes front – stand at ease – stand easy'.

Day in and day out such commands would be bellowed at us. I have written them as they are spelt but many of the words were changed by the DI's own particular intonation, eg left – right became 'ift – eight'. Coupled with the shouts were insults and ridicule, sometimes aimed at us all but regularly at particular individuals. When marching we would be encouraged to 'open our legs' coupled with the information 'we wouldn't lose anything' or threatened to 'swing those arms, before I come over and break them off and flog you to death with the soggy ends'.

Some of the remaining time was taken up by physical training sessions. These were led by the PTIs (physical training instructors) who referred to all basic training airmen as 'dicks'. The rest of the time we attended medicals for vaccinations and innoculations, we had gas lectures, group photographs – in front of the Lancaster, fire lectures and so on. The lectures were pleasant diversions, away from all the marching, running and PE. We usually managed to sit down and if the subject was boring the temperature rise from 120 bodies in the confined space of one of the many huts used as lecture rooms caused us to rapidly fall asleep.

I slept through nearly all of the gas lectures. But, I can remember being told that if nerve gas came in contact with your skin it killed you. I don't know why. Later we all had a session wearing gas masks and taking them off in a tear gas filled enclosure. The gas caused a prickly sensation to the eyes, this led to the tears and much blinking to try and see. Our eyes itched for some hours after the experience.

Some lectures were held in the Astra cinema. Two corporals entertained us one wet afternoon with a description of the various fire appliances and alarms we could expect to find on an RAF Station.

I will remember part of the fire lecture for ever. One corporal was describing a standard fire point made up of an audible alarm, one bell or steel triangle and a hammer to create an audible alarm, and two fire buckets – one filled with water (if maintained properly) and the other bucket filled with sand (the same proviso applying). Usually there was no water in the first bucket and like the sand bucket it would be full of easily combustible items – viz – empty cigarette packets, fag ends, spent matches, crisp packets, bus tickets etc.

While we dutifully laughed at this statement his colleague came onto the stage carrying a fire bucket which he held up and said 'This is a standard issue two gallon galvanised firebucket. Painted red on the outside to denote fire – for those people who can't read – plus fire in black letters for them as can read, but painted white on the inside to denote bullshit.'

Our spare time, the evenings and most weekends, was spent on the 'bull' which the drill instructors insisted was absolutely necessary to keep our billet, our kit and ourselves in a pristine condition.

Back to the billet. Hut Number 123, had two entrance doors, one at each end. The front door faced the road and the parade ground. The back door gave access to three washhouses, at right angles to the billets. They were shared with another nine billets. More than 200 men shared twenty washbasins, six baths, six showers, six urinals and twenty WCs.

Each washhouse had a coke fired vertical boiler which provided hot water for only as long as the boiler fire was stoked. A boiler firing rota was one of the first priorities after we moved into the billet. The boilers needed stoking every three hours day and night. Anyone who failed to ensure the boiler provided hot water had a consecutive stint on the rota, as well as a lot of abuse from his fellows.

The billet had two small rooms, one on either side of the front door. One was a storeroom, the other was the DI's bunk and refuge. The rest of the billet contained twenty beds and one rifle rack. The wall space between

23

the windows of the hut contained the bed spaces. Everyone had a bed-space, approximately five feet wide by eight feet long. The bedspace contained the bed and a similar area alongside the bed, several coat hooks on the wall behind the bed, a shelf above the coat hooks and a wooden kitbox at the foot of the bed.

The kitbox was a wooden ex-ammunition box, varnished inside and painted gloss black outside. The bed frame was made of steel angle and contained a steel wire mesh supported on a number of springs. The frame was painted gloss black. On the steel wire mesh were three 'biscuits' – a biscuit was a mattress about two feet six inches square and three inches thick. When the biscuits were laid end to end they formed the mattress.

During the day the biscuits were stacked on top of each other at the head of the bed. The four blankets were then folded so that the last blanket was wrapped around the first three which were stacked vertically, while showing only one folded edge of each blanket. The folded blankets were then positioned on top of the biscuits. The pillow, a round object, about two feet long and eight inches in diameter, as hard as iron was placed behind the blanket stack.

The shelf, above the bed, displayed the large pack, small pack and tin helmet. The packs were lined with cardboard scrounged from any source, so that they appeared square. They were also blancoed and the brass fittings were polished.

The coat hoots were not empty, the number one dress uniform, pressed and on a hanger, the buttons polished and fastened, the belt buckle was similarly treated. The great coat hung alongside, with buttons fastened and polished, the sleeves were folded round the back and slipped into the half belt. A scrounged bed spring also linked the pockets together across the back of the coat. As well as giving a slim look to the coat, the spring made it less bulky when carrying it over the arm. The spare beret, with polished badge hung on another hook. The webbing crossbelts and bayonet frog, blancoed and brasses polished were hung beside the uniform and greatcoat.

The ammunition box eventually contained various items of clothing wrapped on to strips of cardboard or wood so that several different coloured strips of cloth were displayed. At each end were rolled up socks. One's razor, shaving brush, toothbrush, toothpaste and soap container rested on top of the strips. For each day's billet inspection the boxes were open. The eating irons – knife, fork, spoon, together with the tea mug were displayed on top of the folded blankets.

The floor under and around the bedspace comprised scrubbed floorboards covered with odd loose pieces of highly polished cork linoleum, once upon a time the whole billet floor had been covered with lino. But austerity was still the order of the day and new lino was not a high government priority.

The remaining kit which was not on immediate display was stored in one's kitbag, which stood on the floor next to the bed head. At bedtime each day items needed for the following day were stacked in order of use in the kitbag. If PT followed the first morning session of square bashing, the PT kit would be at the top of the bag. Every step was taken to ensure that you would not be the last one out of the billet or do something which drew the DI's attention to you.

Every so often a full kit inspection would be held. This entailed laying out every piece of clothing and equipment on the bed. The layout had to follow the standard pattern and any deviations from it immediately landed one with some time-consuming fatigue. A similar punishment was handed out if the inspecting officer or NCO considered an item of kit was not clean.

Later, on permanent station the inspecting officer smashed half the tea mugs in the billet because the glaze was crazed. He said he did it because in his opinion we could all catch gingivitis - gum rot – and as a result could lose all our teeth. A little knowledge is a dangerous thing.

A replacement mug cost one shilling and sixpence (7½p), I wonder if he had shares in a Stoke pottery or the NAAFI.

5

Bull

The original reason for bull was probably to ensure that the troops remained clean and therefore healthy and probably the second reason was that someone deduced that it could also be used to instil discipline into an unruly mob or to permanently dull the brains of the rest. This thinking probably led to the appearance of something between a human being and an animal called drill instructors or the dreaded DIs, whose brains were only programmed to recognise diversions from their very bent standards.

Clean clothes, a clean bed and a clean room, together with clean personal habits are generally accepted as the norm by the majority of people today. But RAF DIs norms went to ridiculous limits, wasting thousands of man hours, gallons of metal polish, blanco and paint, as well as tons of boot polish.

The standard issue boots had a ripple finish to the leather uppers and the soles were liberally scattered with half-inch diameter steel studs, plus steel toe and heel plates. These decorations were obviously put there to reduce wear. They also helped to create noise when one performed drill movements. The application of wax polish to the uppers followed by rubbing with a duster to give a shine was not enough for the DIs.

Firstly, the toecaps had to be smooth, not rippled

and secondly, they had to shine like a mirror. If the boots had been ordered with smooth toe caps the need to smooth them out would have been eliminated but the RAF or DIs couldn't think of that simple solution. So we spent hours using a spoon handle and yellow duster to work polish and spittle into the leather to satisfy the DIs demands.

When your toecaps ultimately reflected your face in them it was relatively easy to maintain the shine. Third party damage, the effect of other airmen's boots and equipment on your boots was a major hazard. Scratches and scrapes took time to hide and sometimes the whole glossy toecap would flake off and it was back to the spit and polish again.

If one did not achieve the desired effect, as well as being told to do it again, one ended up doing fatigues. A favourite fatigue of one DI was to clean a particular pane of glass in one of the billet windows. The glass had a blue/green tint and was not as clear as most of the panes. Other windows also contained similar glass but they did not matter. It was this one piece of glass and the fatigue was to clean it to remove the colour cast. That was impossible, so one carried on cleaning it with metal polish until the DI said it was clean. By then precious time had been wasted which could have been spent on one's own kit before going to sleep or down to the NAAFI club.

The RAF employed people to stamp your service number on each item of clothing and equipment when you were issued with it. Then the awkward factor appeared when the DIs wanted the number exactly in the centre of the articles displayed on the kit layouts. The original markings never coincided with their require ments. So one had to invest in ink and tapes, as well as time to sew the numbers onto the kit in the new places.

All webbing had to be blancoed. Blanch means to whiten. Blanco in the services came in all colours – white, blue, black, khaki etc., just another misconception. On basic training our webbing was blue. We had to purchase blue blanco, obtainable from the Naafi canteen, as most of the other cleaning items were. Blanco is a thick paste which was brushed onto the webbing items and brushed until it dried. The brushing made the blanco shine.

The brass items on the webbing had previously been polished and after blancoing they needed touching up. Great care was required to keep the Brasso – metal polish – off the polished webbing. The button stick was a useful aid when cleaning brasses.

Uniforms had to be pressed, the brass badges, buttons and buckles polished. Again care was needed to keep the Brasso off the cloth. The billet floor was scrubbed, the lino polished, the windows cleaned, the washhouses washed down and all were cleaned everyday.

As the weeks of squarebashing progressed nearly every airman ensured that he made the least mess in order to reduce the amount of cleaning required. But the damp autumn air which freely circulated through the for ever open doors and windows of the billets rapidly turned all brass items green.

One other major bull item was the short Lee Enfield Drill Rifle. Every sprog was issued with one. They were incapable of firing a live round, all the firing pins had been filed off. The rifles, minus the bolts, were stored in the locked rifle rack when not being used for rifle drill. Each sprog kept his rifle bolt in his kitbag, for safety and security! The two were only brought together for drill purposes.

The rifle was another piece of equipment to be kept

29

clean. It also came complete with a webbing sling, which had a brass buckle on each end, yet more cleaning.

Yes, just a load of BULL.

☆   ☆   ☆

The Airman's Lament

This is my story, this is my song,
I've been in this air force too blinking long.
You can fly in the air, or work on the ground.
But you'll only get out when your turn comes
    around.

6

Corporal Smith, Drill Instructor

Corporal Smith was the senior drill instructor in our flight. He was about five feet six-inches tall and very solidly built. His turnout each working day was immaculate and he must have spent hours preparing for the moment when he stepped out of his billet, to immediately pull-up some unfortunate airman and point out, with his swagger cane, several short-comings in the airman's turnout.

The corporal's beret appeared to be moulded to his skull, except where the RAF cap badge was supported vertically by a backing plate made out of a Kiwi boot polish tin lid. This support allowed a fold of beret material to hang down the side of his head partially covering the right ear. The small amount of dark hair showing below the beret was close cropped and beginning to turn grey.

His face was round and puffy, with close together pig-like eyes. The nose showed signs of having been flattened several times. The mouth was set in a permanent sneer, broken only when it opened to bellow out a command or to harangue some luckless airman.

The finish to Corporal Smith's battledress would have made any dry cleaning firm green with envy. The jacket had been pressed to show a horizontal crease on the back, across the shoulders and two edge pleats had been formed from the shoulders to the waist. The front of the jacket was also smoothly pressed and each sleeve had a vertical crease to front and rear. The finishing touch was a gleaming white lanyard looped around the left shoulder, with the loose end disappearing into the left breast pocket.

The trousers with knife edge creases were enclosed at the ankles in short, blue blancoed, webbing puttees. The trouser bottoms contained chains to give a symmetrical roll of material over the puttees. Around his waist a standard webbing belt. The belt, like the puttees was finished in pale blue polished blanco, the brass fittings on all these items, as well as the cap badge, were all highly polished. The final items were his boots, with the toe caps polished like glass and good enough to use as a mirror for shaving.

This was the sight we would see every morning as we ran out of the billet and were yelled at to 'get fell in'. The other drill instructors tried to emulate him, but they did not manage to completely match him. Smith was lord above all and when he gave commands he was probably heard by ships' crews on the Manchester Ship Canal to the south, or by lorry drivers on the East Lancs trunk road to the north.

The drill instructors would change command of flights as Corporal Smith directed and my flight was taken over by him one afternoon for rifle drill. On that morning several of us, including myself, had had some additional diptheria injections and by the time we were on parade my left arm was becoming quite stiff and painful.

We 'got fell in' on the road, were marched to the drill square and after several manouevres we achieved 'open order' with rifles at the 'slope'. Open

32

order is when the flight is in three ranks and the front and rear ranks have each moved two paces away from the centre rank; the opposite state is 'close order'. I was in the rear rank. We were facing the front so that Smithy could see everyone.

The 'slope' position, is when the rifle is resting on the left shoulder, with the butt supported by the left hand and the left forearm is parallel with the ground.

Corporal Smith yelled 'order arms', the drill movement to get the rifle across the body so that it is then held at the muzzle by the right hand, with the butt now resting on the ground at the side of the right boot.

Simplicity itself: lower the left arm and hand to partly lower the rifle, at the same time bring the right hand across the body and grasp the rifle near the muzzle then swing the rifle across the body placing the butt on the ground adjacent to the right foot. Done to a count of 'one and two and three'. But not today.

When I tried to extend my left arm down the pain from the jab was terrible and my arm only moved halfway, the natural reaction to stop the pain. Meanwhile the sudden cessation of arm movement caused the rifle to bounce off my shoulder. When the right hand arrived the rifle had gone, the hand only slapped my shoulder.

The rest of the flight had completed the order, when about one second later my rifle completed it's trip through space and hit the deck muzzle first and then bounced onto the butt, then back to muzzle and seemed to continue to oscillate in this mode for several seconds. I remained where I was, Standing to attention and minus one rifle. To have moved to pick it up would only have compounded the existing problem.

The noise created by a drill Short Lee Enfield .303 rifle hitting the ground is very loud indeed. The sound died away. I remained standing at attention, trying to bring my left fore-arm to the side of my body. Everyone was now watching Corporal Smith, he stood absolutely still, his feet at ten to two, he appeared to be frozen to the spot. He didn't move, his face was twitching, he was trying to restrain himself.

But the opportunity to bawl out an airman was too good to miss. He took off and marched through the ranks. One end of his swagger cane tucked into his left armpit the other end gripped tightly in his left hand. His right arm swinging forward and up to shoulder height with the thumb rigid on top of his clenched fist. Finally, he thundered to a halt, six-inches away from me. I was praying that the ground should swallow me up. No such luck.

Since, I was taller than him and he had come so close his cap badge was directly in front of my eyes. From this viewpoint I could see part of the Kiwi pattern of the boot polish tin lid acting as the backing plate behind his cap badge. Also the eagle and the initials R A F on the badge had been worn smooth by repeated polishing..

I had taken all this in before the mouth below the badge erupted. He refered to the lack of any relationship with my parents, using many expletives and many pints of saliva sprayed at my adams apple. The five minute harangue could be reduced to this abridged version:

Cpl Smith: 'You 'orrible illigitimate little airman,

34

	you 'ave dropped your "peeping" rifle 'aven't you.' (Stating the obvious).
Me:	'Yes corporal.' (In these situations the less said, in reply, the better, but watch out for the trick question.)
Cpl Smith:	'I'm a "peeping peep" What am I?'
Me:	'You're a corporal, corporal.'

or because he was so close –

Cpl Smith:	'Did you use a mirror when you shaved this morning?'
Me:	deliberate answer this time, 'Yes corporal.'
Cpl Smith:	Expected reply 'Try using a "peep-ing" razor next time.'

If the clever answer had been – 'No corporal, I used a razor', the reply would have been – 'Try using a "peep-ing" mirror as well as a peep-ing razor'.

The Catch 22 situation arose on many occasions. The art of what to answer and when to answer had to be quickly learned or one became a marked man, to be used as an example to all at any opportunity.

The dialogue went on for several more minutes, when he noticed my left arm was stuck out from my body. He immediately tried to push it down to my side. I had earlier tried to tell him it was painful and that was why I had dropped my rifle, but his brain could apparently only retain such information for a very short time. He only ceased trying to use my arm as the village pump handle when a soft voice called out 'Corporal Smith'. It was Station Padre who was standing against his bicycle on the road beside the square.

'Sir' yelled Corporal Smith simultaneously perform-

35

ing an about turn and raising his right arm in salute. With a crash of boots he completed the turn and, marched off the square to join the Padre.

Whilst he stood rigidly to attention the Padre had a one-sided conversation with him. Unfortunately we were too far away to hear it. The Padre finished speaking, Corporal Smith yelled 'Sir' and threw up another of his perfect salutes, where the forearm and hand bounced to rest like an old railway semaphore signal arm.

He about turned and marched back to the front of the flight. He appeared to have lost all interest in the dropped rifle and ordered me to fall out and pick it up. He also ordered anyone else who had had a jab that morning to fall out and stand at the side of the square until the drill period was over.

There is a god you know and he does answer your prayers.

7

'My Friend Malcolm'

The drill instructors always found one unfortunate airman to become an example, usually by ridicule, to impress a particular point on the rest of the squad. On the first day of square bashing Malcolm was selected as the unfortunate one.

Malcolm spoke slowly and precisely with a south Staffordshire accent. He was nearly six feet tall, with long arms and bowed shoulders. His eyebrows were bushy, he led with his jaw and always appeared to need a shave. He also had a degree in Civil Engineering.

It became immediately obvious to the DIs that Malcolm had a problem when he marched. He moved the same leg and arm backwards and forwards in perfect synchronism, whilst every other airman in the squad was moving opposite arms and legs together. Malcolm's odd man out activities led to him being called out of the ranks so that he could demonstrate his technique to the rest of us.

He stood in front of Corporal Brown, who asked him for his name. Unfortunately or deliberately Malcolm gave his christian name, to which the DI reminded him and interspersed it with suitable invective that in the Air Force one was not a person – only a name and number. On subsequent occasions when the DI needed Malcolm's services to show how something should not be done, he always called for 'my friend MALCOLM'.

Note – Marching should not be confused with the civilian pedestrian activity of walking. Marching is a method of moving a mass of men or women from point A to point B as quickly as possible and ensuring that they arrive together, at the same time, the speed varies from 120 to 140 paces per minute.

We, the squad, were ordered to stand fast and Corporal Brown yelled out the order to Malcolm, 'Quick March'. Malcolm sprang into action leading with his chin, his left arm and left leg swinging forward and then backward, while his right arm and leg moved in the opposite direction. As he moved forward the repeated actions gave his body a peculiar swaying motion. After several paces the DI would scream 'halt', and then call Malcolm back to the starting position.

There then followed a period of detailed instruction, coupled with further invective and forced arm and leg movements, intended to show Malcolm and ourselves how it was done. But when the order 'Quick March' was given, Malcolm moved off with the same arm and leg movements as before. Corporal Brown's face became more red and his expletives more blue.

He enlisted the help of other DIs and after several instruction sessions over several days, which included a DI on each side of Malcolm forcing his arm movements to follow the opposite leg, Malcolm eventually adopted the usual style of marching. A smile of satisfaction appeared on the DI's face, he ordered Malcolm 'to get fell in'. But after several paces, following the order to 'quick march', Malcolm fell back to his own original style.

As the weeks passed no amount of individual tuition changed his style of marching, the times when he was pulled out of the squad for ridicule ceased and he was eventually left on the edge of the square. We went on to perfect the drill movements we would have to perform at the passing out parade and later on for the daily, weekly and ceremonial parades during our stay in the RAF.

Malcolm's new talent for standing still was not wasted. The Royal Air Force had a use for everyone, as the day of the passing out parade approached the number of drill parades increased and Malcolm with several other airmen was stood on the square at a fixed position, to act as markers for the turning points for the flights marching and counter-marching on the big day.

The November day arrived and with it thick fog. All kit was packed, everyone knew their next RAF posting. Leave passes and travel warrants to home and the next RAF station were in our pockets. Breakfast was completed and the fog still persisted. Reports that relatives and girl friends were arriving at the square filtered down the billet lines. The final polish was given to boots and brasses. The markers, including Malcolm, were 'fell in' and marched off to take up their positions in the fog.

The command for our flight to fall in, was followed by a rapid inspection and some further dress adjustments. Then 'slope arms', 'left turn' and 'by the right, quick march' and off into the fog to join two flights from Number Two Wing and another from Number One Wing who were also passing out. As we wheeled onto the square one could just about make out about a hundred civilians huddled on seats, wrapped up against the weather.

After coming to a halt, followed by 'left turn' then 'right dress', 'eyes front', the next command was

'General salute, present arms', rifles were brought to the present, boots bashed on tarmac and the band played the RAF Salute. The fog made it very difficult to see the saluting base, or the Air Vice Marshal who was receiving the salute.

After 'order arms' the Reviewing Officer carried out the inspection, stopping to speak to about every twentieth airman. The inspection was followed by a series of marching manouevres accompanied by the station band, which were similar to trooping the colour, but our audience could only see the flight immediately in front of them because of the fog.

The Air Vice Marshal addressed us on the virtues of signing on for a career in the RAF and also how pleased he was to see such a wonderful turnout and a perfect performance. It was during his speech that the fog began to clear and the sun broke through and we could now see the total parade of some 400 plus – officers, NCOs and airmen, including Malcolm and the other markers. We then marched past the saluting base giving a final salute of 'eyes right' and then 'eyes front'. Then wheeling off the parade ground to be dismissed and 'fall out' for the last time at RAF Padgate.

Those airmen who had relatives or friends at the parade went to meet them. The rest of us took our rifles to the armoury. We then said our own goodbyes, picked up our kit bags and climbed aboard one of the waiting Bedford three ton troop carriers to be taken to Warrington Station to go home on leave.

Malcolm was on the same Bedford as myself and he remained standing by the tailboard until the engine started, then he shouted for Corporal Brown. The NCO approached the back of the truck and asked what his 'friend Malcolm' wanted and as the truck started to move away Malcolm gave him a fully extended arm V sign as well telling him the true facts of his birth.

The NCO stood transfixed, unable to retaliate, powerless to inflict any more of his sadism on any of us as the truck turned a corner and he dissappeared from view behind the barrack huts.

Malcolm climbed down from the truck at Warrington Railway Station lifted his kitbag onto his left shoulder and marched off towards the Manchester train swinging his right arm with his left leg and the expression on his face was one of great satisfaction.

8

Physical Training and the Assault Course

A serviceman had to be fit. This was very evident in those eight weeks of Basic Training, where drill instruction was in the open air for several hours each day, and quite a lot of it at the double (running).

Interspersed with the drill activities was PT, led by PTIs – physical training instructors. Today if you saw a group of them together you would think they were male physiotherapists, they all dressed in white sweaters and navy blue trousers. They showed no badges of rank but they were addressed as sergeant. They always called us 'dicks', never airman, just 'dick'.

The physical training included the usual body exercises of bending down to touch ones toes, bending and twisting the trunk to the left and to the right, knees bend and arms stretch, star jumps and squat thrusts and so on. Other more energetic exercises were running and jumping around and over benches, boxes and horses. These activities were to prepare us for the assault course.

The PTIs introduced us to this particular form of torture, not the DIs. They appeared to treat it as their pride and joy, they urged and threatened us dicks to obtain maximum performance and eventually many of us did.

Although most boys have climbed trees and jumped

over or fallen into a stream, the assault course was, at first an unending series of streams, trees, rope ladders, nets, ropes, planks, fences and walls, which rapidly separated the abnormal from the normal. PT kit was worn for the first attempts to conquer the course, later it would be completed in fatigue kit with full webbing, including packs and rifle.

Simple tasks at ground level appeared to be nearly impossible when they had to be performed three feet above ground. Or three feet above three feet of filthy evil looking water stirred up by the last person to fall in.

Walking across a fifteen-foot long, six-inch wide plank supported on thick posts sounds easy until you put a three-foot gap in the middle and space several similar planks four-feet apart, with staggered gaps over the inevitable water and simultaneously send one 'dick' over each plank.

One participant got to the gap and froze, another stopped and tried to jump the gap only to fall into the water – he who hesitates is lost. These attempts are matched by at least two more who also fall in the water, probably distracted by his girations through space. Two made it to the other side, one ran straight across the obstacle as if it never existed, the other still doesn't know why.

Another simple task was to pull yourself along a horizontal rope, once again suspended over water. You are not allowed to hang under the rope, but must straddle yourself over it. Progress on the first half is easy. Due to the sag in the rope you are going down hill but from mid-point it begins to get harder and is uphill, and balance is made more difficult when another 'dick' gets onto the same rope. One or both of you will inevitably end up in the water.

Other obstacles included:–

the wall, ten-feet high – to be climbed over.

the tree walk – a series of horizontal walk-ways on ropes in the trees

barbed wire entanglements – to be crawled under.

hanging tyres, rope ladders, nets and ropes – to be climbed through, or up or over.

several fences and ditches – to be jumped over.

the chasm – to be swung over.

The chasm followed on from the tree walk. It was a simple rope swing across about twelve feet of water. The near vertical take off and landing banks were two to three feet above the water. The trick of getting safely to the other side was to catch the rope, walk away from the chasm letting the rope slip through your hands as you moved away. Then gripping the rope and lifting your legs off the ground, leave the rest to gravity and the pendulum effect, remembering to let go of the rope to land safely on the other side before you began to swing back again.

One day a PTI was calling to a body on the rope to 'let go you dick'. The unfortunate airman had retained his grip on the rope and was hanging more or less stationary in the middle of the chasm. Eventually and in spite of the directions given by the PTI, gravity took over and he slipped off the rope into about three feet of mud rather than water.

The next airman in the queue was Richard. He

44

weighed more than fifteen stone and found most exercise hard going. Since the rope was out in the middle he had to lean out to grab hold of it and this proved his undoing. Eventually he was reasonably well balanced but instead of moving back from the edge he began to move his hands higher up the rope, while his feet remained on the edge of the bank.

As his body and the ground tended towards an angle of forty-five degrees he could no longer hold onto the rope and he fell flat into the 'water' which then proceeded to slowly cover his back, his neck and finally his head. The PTI shouted 'you stupid dick', but Richard was out of hearing at that moment buried in the mud.

The wall was built of brick and had a ledge at five feet on the down side but was sheer on the up side. It was impossible for one person to climb it alone, it needed a minimum of three people. One stood with his back against the wall and cupped his hands. The other two ran at him, in turn, placing one foot in his cupped hands then the other foot on his shoulder, to end up sitting astride the wall, facing each other. They then reached down to the third man and lifted him to the top of the wall. The ledge, on the down side, made the descent easy.

Another obstacle was a group of several old lorry tyres hanging about six feet apart, the lowest four feet off the ground. The simple task was to pass through the centre of each tyre as fast as possible. Easy in PT kit, grab the top of the tyre swing your legs up and through the hole and follow with the rest of your body. Try the same operation in full kit carrying a rifle. Now the only quick way was to dive through the centre, pick oneself up and proceed to the next tyre.

The whole process of going around the course

developed into a competition to see who could complete it in the shortest possible time and in the cleanest condition. But it was still called 'that bloody assault course'.

9

Fuel Supplies and Pay Parades

After basic training some airmen went on to trade
training. I was posted to RAF Melksham in Wiltshire.
It was an Electrical and Instrument School as well as
basic training unit like Padgate. The billets were wood
and asbestos huts arranged in spider groups. The
school, offices, the mess, the NAAFI club and the
square separated the billets from the school. The
lecture rooms were in two long rows, backed by
another row of large equipment storage sheds.

On the journey from Paddington conversations with
other airmen on the train revealed some were going
to the Radio and Radar School at RAF Yatesbury,
and others were going to Melksham. Most of these
were time served electricians, who had already been
classified 'X' or 'Y' Specification by an RAF trade test.

Just to digress, we changed trains for Melksham at
Chippenham from a main line express to one which
consisted of an ex-GWR tank steam engine and two
carriages. The engine was in the middle between the
carriages and attached to one of them was a Harris of
Calne sausage van. This 'push me – pull me' train
combination was a familiar sight while I was in
Wiltshire. Sometimes a United Dairies milk tank was
substituted for the sausage van.

Back to RAF Melksham, the trade classification

meant that a Y specification needed ten weeks further trade training and an X specification only three weeks familiarisation with RAF equipment. The normal training period for an electrical mechanic from scratch was twenty-two weeks, eleven weeks use of tools and another eleven weeks of electrical theory and practice.

The familiarisation was completed in early December but no postings were announced for electrical fitters/mechanics. Some of us spent several weeks in the transit billet waiting for a posting. During this time we carried out various fatigues.

Fatigues were jobs done as a punishment for some small misdemeanour or by men with nothing else to do. We were in the latter category. Our first job was the coal fatigue. The work consisted of filling sacks with coal or coke in the ratio of two sacks of coke to one sack of coal. Each sack contained half a hundred weight (twenty-five kilos), the coke sacks were twice as big as the coal sacks. The filling was done in a barbed wire enclosed compound.

The sacks were loaded onto thirty hundredweight, Karrier Bantam trucks, driven by civilian drivers from the Air Ministry Works Department (AMWD). The sacks in the ratio of two coke to one coal were delivered to the offices and billets. The school lecture rooms were heated from a central boiler house.

Every billet had two cast iron stoves, with a galvanised steel trough type bunker next to the stove. One week's ration for each stove was two sacks of coke and one sack of coal. If the delivery was on Friday the fuel might last until Sunday night.

The transit billet was always warm since deliveries matched our needs, not the usually inadequate ration. This task was eventually taken over by others waiting for a posting and we moved on to do a bit of civil engineering.

Pay Parades

The pay parades at RAF Melksham were not fatigues but they felt like one. Some of the large equipment sheds at the back of the school were used to store and display aircraft, seaplane tenders, air-sea rescue launches and ground electrical equipment. One contained a collection of German Second World War jet and rocket aircraft. The weekly pay parades were held every Thursday in the sheds.

In one shed cash was paid out to those whose names started with A through to M and the second dealt with those N to Z. I was in the second shed. Hundreds of airmen were marched into the building for 10.00 hours.

A pay clerk called out the first name 'Nabarro', it was answered by a shout of 'Sir, 574' a stamp of feet and the airman marched through the standing masses to the pay table, saluted the paying officer with his right hand, received his pay in his left, made an about turn and marched away from the pay table and out the building. Immediately after Nabarro, Nabbs name was called, then the next and so on and so on. Airmen were moving constantly forward to the table saluting, collecting cash and leaving.

It was ages before the waiting parade of airmen began to thin out and yet more time before only a handful remained, including Vincent, Vokes, Wade, West, Wicks, and me Woodrup. After me came Wyatt, Yates, Yeatman and Young; I could hear their names being called as I left the building at about 12.30 hours.

On permanent station we just turned up at the Workshops Squadron Office, were paid by the Squadron WO and then signed for it.

10

Civil Engineering

The AOC's (Air Office Commanding) annual inspection of RAF Melksham was due. An AOC's inspection is carried out in great depth so that he can check that everything under his command is tickety boo. But it also involved loads of bull and a massive diversion of resources.

Someone in high places had decided that some of the service roads at RAF Melksham were a little tatty because they lacked kerbstones. One must remember this was in early 1952 and austerity was still the order of the day.

Where would the kerbstones come from? That same person in high places had the answer. Remove every other kerbstone on those roads which had kerbstones and then relay them at one yard intervals on the roads which didn't have kerbstones. And why not use the spare men in transit to do the job.

Eight of us from the transit billet formed this fatigue party. We were given KD overalls, two wheelbarrows and a number of picks, shovels, crowbars and a brush, and told off to start at the main entrance to the station.

We arrived at the appropriate spot and proceeded to attack the second kerbstone in from the gate. At that moment in time not one of us had a clue of how a kerbstone was installed. But this lack of knowledge was soon to be rectified.

The kerbstone resisted a frontal attack, which only managed to remove some of the adjacent tarmac. Someone suggested digging up the close cropped turf behind the stone to have a look see. This eventually showed a sloping concrete backing to the stone, which when broken away along the length of the stone, enabled the stone to be pushed backwards into the excavation and then levered out of the hole using a crowbar. Easy when you know how.

Our success, however, was cut short by the appearance of an RAF Police Sergeant screaming at us to 'peeping well stop what we were doing'. We informed him what our instructions were, he again told us to 'peeping well desist' and to wait for further instructions.

We found a sunny spot out of the wind at the side of the guardroom; sat down, smoked and nattered for about an hour. We then decided it was time for a NAAFI break and told the 'snoop' in the guardroom where we could be found and left for the NAAFI club.

On our return we found several senior NCOs, the SWO and the Station Adjutant surveying the site of our earlier activities. The sergeant who gave us the original instructions now told us to re-instate the area we had excavated, putting the kerbstone back in place, and to leave it showing as little damage as possible. He then directed us to the new and agreed starting point, this was further down the road and away from the guardroom and station headquarters.

We spent the rest of the day making good our earlier work and this included a specific directive to water the turf. This was in January, with frosts most nights.

We spent the next four weeks removing alternate kerbstones. The work was interrupted first by snowstorms and then the death of King George VI. This last event led to a lot of parades in three inches of very wet slushy snow, complete with black armbands and muffled drums.

After the King's funeral it was back to the kerbstone fatigue once more. Another difficulty arose and this was finding sufficient soil to fill the holes left when the stones were removed. Eventually the AMWD provided soil by the lorry load. Their trucks also moved the recovered stones to their new sites.

The relaying process was much easier than the removal, although some below ground obstructions occasionally caused short term problems.

Ultimately all the stones had been planted and all the roads had a similar appearance, apart from around the main gate and station headquarters.

Our labours still needed the final touch – Paint. Paint was one item which was never in short supply. We received several five gallon tins of white paint, one tin of black paint and several paint brushes together with the instruction to paint the kerbstones at the main gate and around station headquarters alternately black and white and all other kerbstones white.

It will never be known if the colour scheme was for safety or bull but it fits the old service adage :

> 'if it moves – SALUTE IT'
> 'if you can move it – MOVE IT'
> 'and if you can't move it – **PAINT IT**'

On the actual day of the inspection, in March, all personnel in the transit billet were given a leave pass for the day and told to be off the station from 09.00 hours to 21.00 hours.

Bath is a very interesting and beautiful city if you have several hours to spend finding out!

I was posted to RAF Horsham St Faiths in March 1952. I had never heard of the place. I thought of Horsham in Sussex, but Horsham St Faiths is in Norfolk. The airfield is now Norwich Airport, some of the hangars and the buildings, including Station HQ are an industrial estate, and the domestic site is part of the University of East Anglia.

An AOC'S inspection at Horsham St Faiths led to the airmen's mess and the NAAFI club being prettied up with potted plants on the window sills and pictures on the walls. The final touch was a liberal coat of red cardinal polish on the tiled floors.

On inspection day, some airmen queued for up to three hours for lunch. This was caused by restricting the numbers in the mess at any one time and the tables being cleaned after each use before anyone could sit at them.

A dance was held in the NAAFI club and the dividing doors to the mess were opened to increase the floor area. The station dance band provided the music. Airmen attending had to wear Number One dress, the WAAFs could wear frocks. Nurses from a nearby hospital and girl friends helped to increase the number of partners. 'Mine was alright, but I don't like yours'!

Have you ever tried to dance a foxtrot or a waltz on sticky red cardinal polish, I can tell you it is not easy. The red polish finished up all over your shoes, on the bottom of your trouser legs. It was also on the girls dancing shoes and around their ankles. This arose from having to step around the floor, rather than gliding across it. The dance was not a raving success, when compared with previous ones.

Norwich is another beautiful and interesting city. The locals said it had 365 pubs, fifty-two churches – including the Cathedral and twelve cinemas and theatres. One for each month, week and day of the year. The city also has a castle, many museums and art galleries.

Alas, there was never enough time or money to prove whether it had 365 pubs, but the other two statistics were more or less right. Many of the churches are now museums, art galleries or social centres.

11

Home – the Billet

At RAF Melksham the billets were five star huts when compared with those we had left at RAF Padgate. The huts were clad on the outside with asbestos sheets, lined inside with plasterboards and obviously insulated between these two layers. The floors were brown asphalt and highly polished. Heating was from two cast iron stoves, spaced down the centre line of the hut.

The huts were in groups of eight, four on either side of the ablution block, and they were referred to as 'spiders'. Hot water (if you got up early enough) was on tap, access was by enclosed link passageways. This was luxury in deep mid-winter. Also you could visit friends in other huts without going outside. I had two ex-school friends in the same spider.

Although we were in a training school , bull was still practised and kit as well as the billet had to be cleaned. To polish the billet floor everyone had 'bumpers', these were pieces of thick felt which you stood on and slid around the floor, several of us practiced our dancing technique whilst polishing the floor - slow, slow, quick, quick, slow.

At weekends the hut was completely changed. Many of the occupants went off on weekend passes and those left arranged their pits radially around the stove(s). Nearly all weekend activity, apart from eating and external entertainment, was performed in a horizontal position. This was generally the result of the prevailing cash situation. Life in the transit billets followed a similar pattern.

RAF Horsham St Faith was completely different. The arrival procedure having been completed and our place of work and method of working identified, we moved our kit from transit to the shift 'H' block. That was the middle one on the south side of the square. We shared a top billet with other shift electricians, GCA unit staff, air traffic staff and telephone operators.

The 'H' block took its name from the plan view – the letter H. It was a two storey brick and concrete building. On the ground floor entrance doors in each long side of the H gave access to an entrance hall and two large billets on each side, as well as two NCOs' rooms. Connecting each entrance hall was a corridor across the centre of the H which had bathrooms, showers, wash basins, lavatories, storerooms and drying and ironing rooms on each side of it.

Staircases from the entrance hall led up to the first floor which reflected and duplicated the layout below. Our new billet was about fifty feet long and twenty-five feet wide, with three double windows in each long wall. The windows on the right of the door looked out onto and across the square, The left hand windows faced the billet on the other leg of the H.

The billet had been designed to house upto twenty airmen, but was home to thirty, with the generous use of double bunks and not very many single beds. Ron and I had the double bunk in the right hand corner facing up the room. Our other furniture was two wardrobes and two bedside lockers. The wardrobes stood side by side from the corner and the lockers were stacked one on top of the other between the bunk and the wardrobes, and just to make things more awkward all the doors were hung on the left.

Each airman had a wardrobe and a locker. The other furniture was a table and six chairs, one rifle rack, a 'Tannoy' loudspeaker mounted on the wall above the door, and a rented steam radio. The radio was our contact with the outside world via the Goon Show. It was paid for by the occupants, together with a cash contribution to the Air Ministry for the electricity it consumed. Very little in the Air force was free.

The table legs were attached to the top by a bolt and wing nut. When taken off one leg made a reasonable cricket bat. For a ball we used rolled up polythene bags held together with many rubber bands. Indoor cricket was played regularly. The ball was soft and yet hard enough to break lamp shades and lamps, as well as leaving contact marks on the ceiling and walls. Barrack damage charges were quite high at times.

This billet and two similar ones in the same block were my home for the next seventeen months, except for periods of leave and the odd detachment. During this time the thirty occupants were constantly changing as airmen were demobilised or were posted away to another station and new faces filled the bed spaces.

One new face, an ex RAF apprentice, arrived at the height of the summer and was only in the ground floor billet for two nights. On his first night he easily dropped off to sleep, on his back, and immediately kept everyone awake with a very loud snore as he breathed in and an extremely high pitched whistle when he breathed out. Attempts to turn him on his side gave a short respite. But all failed when he rolled onto his back again. Most of the billet were still awake at dawn and as a result had an early breakfast.

The next night the snoring and whistling filled the

air and once again most of the billet was wide awake. A discussion of the Noise Abatement Society followed on what action should be taken to improve our immediate environment. Suggestions like MURDER and SUFFO-CATION, came top of the list, but it was agreed to remove him, bed and all from the room.

The table and chairs were cleared from the middle of the room and beds on each side of the offending one were also moved to allow for clear unimpeded movement. Eight bods spaced themselves, four on each side and on a hushed count of three lifted the bed up and moved it out of the bedspace and turned to move down the middle of the room.

The turning movement was nearly completed when the snoring abruptly ceased. The carriers lowered the bed, expecting you know who to be awake, but he just turned over and commenced snoring once more. The carriers picked up the bed again and carried it out into the entrance hall.

All those involved climbed into bed hoping to have some sleep. It was not to be, the snores and whistles could still be heard as loud as before, they reverberated and echoed around the entrance hall, staircase and corridors. It was decided he had to go outside. It was a warm night.

We were joined in the hall by bods from the billet opposite who had been awakened by the noise. The bed was lifted up, carried out of the front door, across the corner of the square and put down by the blast shelter at the entrance to the airmens' mess. Someone placed his mug and irons by the bed so he could have his breakfast. We finally got to bed about 01.15 hours.

At about 05.30 hours we were all awake again. The now very irate and wide awake snorer had returned to the billet and had started to tip out of bed as many people as he could before he was forcibly stopped. He left the billet to go to work, moved his kit out at lunchtime and found another billet to terrorise. We who were left enjoyed many peaceful nights.

It later transpired that an airman returning from air traffic, on his bike, cycling down the footpath in front of the NAAFI and the mess, turned right and crashed straight into a bed containing a sleeping snoring airman, who, when fully awake did not really want to be first in the queue for breakfast.

12

Flying Station Organisation and Work

RAF Horsham St Faith was the base for two squadrons
of Gloster Meteor Mark VIII single seater day fighters
and two squadrons of night fighters – one of NF 10
aircraft and one of NF 11 aircraft – De Havilland
Vampire and Gloster Meteor variants. It was also
home to over 3,000 airmen and airwomen, NCOs and
Officers.

Number Twelve Group Fighter Command Headquarters was also located on the station. This meant
that one had to ensure that salutes were given to staff
vehicles displaying pennants and stars, even when only
the driver was in it.

The station commander was a group captain. The
next command level was three wings – flying wing,
technical wing and administration wing. Each wing
was under the command of a wing commander. The
title of the wings was a general description of their
responsibilities.

Flying wing included the squadrons and station
flight. Station flight looked after visiting aircraft and
three Tiger Moths, several gliders, three Meteor Mark
VII two seater trainers, two Beaufighters and the CO's
Auster. The Beaufighters, which were unserviceable
had been used as target tugs but proved too slow for
the Meteors.

Technical Wing provided technical services to both the flying wing and the administrative wing. These included transport, ground power services, photography and gun camera film processing, electrical and instrument services, aircraft tyre and brake services, armaments, engines, etc.

The administrative wing as well as providing pay and rations also looked after security – by the RAF Police and guards drawn from all the wings, it was responsible for obtaining, holding and distributing stores, the station fire service also came under it's wing.

The station adjutant's office was responsible for the normal running of the station and all ceremonial duties. The actual detail for guards and for most ceremonial parades was delegated to the station warrant officer – the SWO.

Every airman on arriving at a new station had to go through the arrival procedure. This usually started on the day after he arrived. At the station adjutant's office he was given a card which listed every wing office, every squadron office, every section office, and in some cases sub-section offices. The list was on both sides of the card, with an adjacent blank column for signature. The card also contained one's name, rank, number, wing, squadron and section.

Armed with the card you had to visit every place listed and obtain the signature of the senior officer or the senior NCO to show you had been there and could possibly remember where it was at some future date. Another card was similarly filled in when you were permanently leaving the station. It was used to ensure that you only left with what you had initially brought onto the station.

The visiting could take as long as you wanted, you did not exist on station strength until the completed card was returned to the SWO's office. I went into the office, waited and was eventually seen by the 'SWOMAN', he signed my card and then asked

'Airman how tall are you?'

'Five foot nine sir' I replied.

'Good, you are just the man I want, you are now a member of the guard of honour for as long as you remain on station.'

I was given a chit to take to the stores and draw one white webbing belt, one white webbing bayonet frog and one white webbing rifle sling. I also had to buy some white blanco for extra bull. The RAF didn't provide it. I later discovered that an airman of similar height who had been in the Guard of Honour was demobbed the day I arrived so I was filling his place.

The station was divided into two areas – the domestic site and the technical site. The first contained the billets, the airmens' mess and NAAFI club, the sergeants' mess, the officers' mess, married quarters and the NAAFI shop. The latter included the workshops, hangars, stores, transport depot, sick quarters, the fuel and bomb dumps, the runways, taxi tracks and servicing strip or apron. The strip was a huge rectangle of concrete, which provided parking for over 100 aircraft.

I arrived at Horsham St Faiths with Ron, another electrical mechanic, at 18.15 hours after travelling up from Melksham. The Corporal snoop on duty at the guardroom told us to grab our 'irons' and go to the mess immediately or we would miss tea. The mess closed at 18.30 hours.

We asked him to look after our kitbags and followed his directions to the mess. The mess looked like its name. The tables were littered with slices of bread, with dirty plates here and there covered with the remains of butter and jam. Two airmen were still eating and having a football argument.

We approached the servery, plates in hand. A cook scraped a ladle around in a huge aluminium bowl. When he lifted it up the ladle contained a glutinous, yellowish, lumpy mass.

The cook inverted the ladle over my plate and the mass slowly detached itself and descended, splodge, onto the plate. I looked at this delicacy, I smelled it and decided that as well as looking revolting it smelled revolting. I enquired

'What is it?'

The cook replied 'Macaroni cheese.'

I walked straight over to the slop bin and tipped the slumping revolting mess into it. I added the plate to one stack of the many dirty ones piled up beside the bin. My first tea at Horsham was bread and jam, and a pot of tea. The two airmen were still arguing about football as we left the mess.

We spent the night in the transit billet and started the 'arrival' procedure the next day, collecting our cards and beginning the grand tour of the station. It took two days to obtain the necessary signatures.

Looking from the strip part of the technical site layout consisted of a row of three hangars. Numbered two, three and four from right to left, behind number two and four hangars were hangars one and five. Hangars one to four housed the day and night fighter squadrons, and station flight occupied number five hangar. Single storey offices, air-crew rooms and workshops were attached to the front and back of each hangar.

The stores, technical wing headquarters and station workshops were in the space between one, three and five hangars. Behind number one hangar was the transport section workshops and garages. Sick quarters was behind number five hangar.

After arriving we reported to Chiefy in the electrical section office at Number two hangar. Chiefy told us we would start in the acc-room. Because the station had night fighters it meant working shifts. We went over to the acc-room at Number three hangar to meet Robbo and Johnny. They told us the shift pattern was twenty-four hours on and twenty-four hours off, two men covering each period. The section provided relief cover for leave etc. The acc-room supplied new and recharged accumulators (batteries) for aircraft, aircraft starter trollies (trolley-accs), heavy vehicles and cars, ground portable power supplies and generators.

Reveille was at 06.30 hours – a record of a bugle blowing reveille – broadcast over the tannoy. The 'day workers' working day started at 07.45 hours, when they 'fell in' for the working parade after which they were marched off to their various offices and sections, to start work at 0800 hours. Shift workers did not attend the working parade since they had to relieve the previous shift. Generally we worked flexible start and finish shift times to suit our personal arrangements or those of the opposite shift.

The Meteor day fighters were towed out from the hangars onto the strip and parked in ranks with sufficient space between the ranks to allow the aircraft to turn and taxi off or onto the strip. Other equipment, fire extinguisher sets, trolley-acc power trailers and their Triumph generator sets were also towed out in long strings and dispersed between the aircraft.

The trolley-accs were plugged into the aircraft. Various trades from the A and B flights of the squadrons carried out pre-flight checks on the aircraft. If it was pronounced O.K it was ready to fly. If an aircraft was declared unserviceable work was either

65

carried out on the strip or the aircraft was towed back to the hangar for the Squadron C flight to rectify the problem. Petrol bowsers (tankers) also moved between the parked aircraft dispensing aviation fuel.

The pilots came out from the crew rooms after briefing. The pilot checked his aircraft externally, removed the pitot head cover sleeve and climbed up to and into the cockpit. He removed the safety pin and disk from the ejector seat firing mechanism and stowed it in the clip behind the seat. He then turned and sat down in the seat. A rigger or mechanic attendant helped him fasten his seat harness and then climbed down to ground level.

The rigger stood to the port side of the aircraft's nose while the pilot went through the engine starting routine. The pilot signalled to the rigger who switched the aircraft electrics from ground to aircraft supply, he unplugged the trolley-acc and pushed it away from the aircraft. The rigger then moved to near the port wing tip to wait for the pilot's signal to remove the wheel chocks. In all his ground movements the rigger kept well away from the port engine nacelle air intakes.

On seeing the pilot's signal the rigger pulled on the chock chains, when they were clear of the wheels he stood clear of the port wing and the pilot moved the aircraft forward out of the rank of parked aircraft, turned ninety degrees to starboard to leave the strip and join the taxi-track to go round to the runway in use that day. The runway in use was dictated by the wind direction and speed.

Meanwhile the rigger had picked up the wheel chocks, stowed them on the trolley-acc and had moved on to the next aircraft. When all his aircraft were dispatched the trolley-accs were connected to the generators for recharging.

66

On a hot summer's day the conditions on the strip were like Dante's Inferno. The scream of tortured air being compressed with fuel and burned to drive the turbines, which in turn drove the compressors still faster in the aircraft's jet engines, the heat from the sun and exhaust gases, smoke from engines, the smell of vaporised paraffin, and danger from moving aircraft and jet pipe exhaust gas streams.

Returning aircraft were guided by their attendant rigger into a space on the strip. The pilot would cut the engines and the turbines would take several minutes to stop rotating and more time to cool down. Chocks were placed against the wheels. The pilot replaced the ejector safety pin in the seat firing mechanism and climbed down to the ground. Informed the rigger of any problems, replaced the pitot head cover and went off to debriefing and to take a rest. Meanwhile, a trolley-acc had been plugged in and the ground crew tradesmen were carrying out their post flight checks.

This process went on throughout the day, aircraft being prepared to fly, aircraft taxiing, aircraft taking off, aircraft landing, aircraft taxiing back to the strip, aircraft being post-flight checked, aircraft being refuelled (and rearmed when on target exercises) and aircraft being pre-flight checked to fly again. The same continued into the night as the day fighters were replaced by the night fighters.

The need for aircraft ground electrical supplies meant the trolley-accs were recharged by the Triumph generators several times each day. When they failed to recharge the trolley-accs were brought to the acc-room where a quick check would indicate a short circuited cell in one of the four six-volt batteries in the trolley. Remove and replace the faulty battery. Check state of charge, trolley-acc ready for service again.

Aircraft supplies were met by generators on each engine and two twelve-volt forty-ampere hour lead acid batteries located in the nose wheel bay under the pilots feet. The batteries were secured on trays which were locked into the battery compartment by spring loaded bolts. If they needed changing it took only a few minutes to release and exchange them for a freshly charged set.

Note: the trolley-acc was a twenty-four volt 240 ampere hour battery – four six-volt 240 ah lead acid batteries connected in series. Compared with a typical car battery rating of twelve volt – thirty or forty ampere hour the power output of the trolley-acc was greater by six to eight times.

13

On Station Sports Activities

The services gave as much assistance as possible to anyone who wanted to participate in their chosen sport. Such as – all football, hockey and rugby strips were provided and laundered by the PT staff, cash assistance was given for the purchase of boots and time was made available for the games to be played. This was every Wednesday afternoon and additional time off normal duties was always available.

When I was stationed near Norwich as many as ten football teams, one hockey team and one rugby team turned out every Wednesday.

I played rugby. The team was made up of officers and other ranks, in more or less equal numbers. Also a similar division between rugby union and rugby league players existed in the team, but we did not dwell on the fact. The full back was a league player and his perfect distance kicking saved a lot of running about as well as converting a lot of goals. The team would not have existed if these players had not been available.

The team played as RAF Horsham St Faiths on Wednesdays and some Saturdays. On the other Saturdays some of us played for Norwich Extra Firsts. The team had a full fixture list and played against other clubs in Norfolk, Suffolk and Cambridgeshire, against other RAF teams, Army and Navy Base teams, as well as college and Town Rugby Clubs. The RAF Cup games led to extra matches, not always on a Wednesday or a Saturday. We also practised on two evenings each week, and were very fit.

The only time I scored an allowed try in my whole rugby career was during a Saturday match at Sudbury in Suffolk. The Sudbury Club's headquarters was a pub. The pitch was outside the town and the cows had been taken off it half an hour before the kick-off. I played blind side loose forward, flanker today, and Taff Woodruff played open side loose forward. In the line outs Taff and I were at the tail.

On this particular day my opposite number in the line was about six inches taller and about a couple of stones heavier than me. Also he had a nasty habit of ramming his elbow into my ribs when I went up for the long ball. After a while my ribs began to get sore and my temper was getting shorter.

He then started complaining when my boot regularly contacted his shin. We agreed that he would stand forward so that bodily contact was reduced. He went forward I went further back and on one line out, about ten yards from their line, a long ball came straight into my hands. Somehow I went between the opposing scrum-half, stand-off and full back, flying through the air into the biggest freshest cowpat on the field.

To add insult to injury the press report gave the try to Taff Woodruff.

After the match we returned to the pub, shared the very hot communal bath then enjoyed some good food, consumed some beer and started playing darts with the locals.

Darts was a very popular game in the Norfolk pubs. The heavy brass darts with plastic fletches were not allowed, they had to be wooden darts with lead weights and feather fletches.

All reasonable players carried their own set of darts and the team was no exception. My personal set were called 'sissy darts', because they were like pencils with feathers.

As the evening went by the locals lost the matches and bought the beer. They were upset when we had to leave and as we settled down on the coach for the journey back to Norwich the pub landlady appeared on the steps accusing us of having taken a set of the pub's darts.

The thief she said was dressed in a blue blazer and grey slacks. Eighteen people on the coach, including the driver stood up and offered to be searched. The popular garb then was blue blazers and grey slacks. The landlady gave up and we departed into the night.

Mania

Canasta, the card game, was all the rage and during lunchtimes and evenings the NAAFI canteen tables would be fully occupied by canasta playing groups. At this time Ron, Johnny and I had an imaginary cat, Charlie. We adopted him after seeing James Stewart in 'Harvey'.

During our canasta games we always had a spare chair for Charlie to sleep on. If any bod asked if 'He could take the chair?' he would be told 'No, it's Charlie's'. They probably thought he was at the bar.

Charlie even went to the pictures with us. After one visit to the cinema we boarded a late bus in Castle Meadow. The top deck of the double decker had rows of seats for four passengers and a side aisle. Ron and

Johnny sat on the window side seats and I sat on the end next to the aisle, there was space for Charlie between us.

The conductress shouted from the platform 'Is the top deck full?' Someone said 'Yes', she rang the bell and the bus moved off. Eventually the conductress came to collect the fares. When she came to our seat, she pointed to the empty seat, saying she had been told it was full! I said 'It wasn't empty, Charlie our cat was on it'. She then gave me two tickets – one full fare for me and half fare for Charlie.

14

Training for War Games

All airmen were supposed to complete a one week ground combat training course every year. The course was led and supervised by members of the RAF Regiment.

Since most of my first year on the station was spent as a shift worker I, along with many others, was excused certain duties. These duties included – guards, duty electrician, working parades and on station courses.

One day our two night fighter squadrons flew away to pastures new. The powers that be decided it was no longer necessary to have shift workers providing a service which no one wanted after 18.00 hours – six p.m. Our immunity to extra duties ceased immediately.

One could hear the shout of joy from the station warrant officer's office as he drew up new guard rosters using several hundred names he couldn't include before. Station Orders soon showed my name on guard duty as well as having to attend a ground combat training course, 'GCT' for short.

A 'working' parade of all personnel intending to work was held at 07.45 hours every working day, except Wednesday, and each section commander inspected his section before marching them off to their work places. We now had to attend working parades, complete with overalls, battle-dress ironed, cap badge polished and boots bulled.

One Monday morning after the 'working' parade, about thirty airmen including myself, complete with rifles, tin hats, eating irons, mess tins and KD overalls clambered aboard a three-ton Bedford troop carrier. The truck left the parade ground and followed the taxi track round to the far side of the airfield, where it stopped outside a Nissen hut. We climbed down to be met by two RAF Regiment sergeants.

Behind the solitary Nissen hut the ground stretched away to the perimeter fence and it looked like no man's land. It was complete with slit trenches, craters, sand bags, barbed wire and all sorts of debris. The area in front of the Nissen hut had short grass on it and a well-defined path crossed the grass to the hut door.

One of the sergeants got us to fall in, a roll call showed all present and correct. The other sergeant then outlined the next five days' activities. These included lectures on the fighting role of the RAF Regiment and how we soldiers – not airmen – would fit into the scheme of things if war came.

We would also practice the art of camouflage, wire laying and cutting, placing mines and setting booby traps as well as detecting same. A day would be spent at the rifle range, firing the rifle, Sten gun and the Bren gun.

The talk over, the command 'attention', followed by 'right turn', and the instruction 'in single file, front rank leading', and the commands 'quick march, left wheel' led the column onto the path towards the hut. After about thirty paces there was a loud explosion and clouds of dense white smoke. We stopped moving only to be immediately ordered to march on into the hut.

As the leading airman opened the door there was another huge explosion and masses of white smoke billowed out of the hut. The column stopped once more and a very amused sergeant pushed past and led the way into one room, containing a table, two blackboards and several rows of chairs.

The two laughing sergeants sat down and asked us to do the same. We did and as thirty bottoms descended onto chairs several more explosions shook the air and the room filled with smoke. Through the fog a sergeant shouted 'open the windows'. Someone did. Yet another explosion. By now we were laughing with the sergeants. Loud bangs were normal and amusing.

When the smoke eventually cleared we were told that if the booby traps had been real bombs the majority of us would be dead. We were now soldiers in a war situation and had to act as such. Our instructors then explained the explosions were caused by a trigger device firing a detonator, which in turn ignited a short length of fuse. The detonator produced the bang and the fuse the smoke.

The device could be selected to use either compression or expansion to operate the trigger. It also had a ring to allow trip wires to be fastened to it, another way of firing it.

On being told to look for them, several were found, one by the door, another by the window and more under the chairs. The device was the size of a matchbox and was two metal plates, joined by a hinge to form a box shape. The box was kept open or forced open by a spring. The hinge mechanism drove the firing pin. The device could be fired either by pressure closing it tight or by flying open when the pressure was released.

Instruction then followed on how to fit the detonator and fuse and drawings of this were made on one of the blackboards. The sergeant also listed the speed of the different coloured fuses. He then asked one of the airmen in the front row to turn the blackboard over and he would see how much we had retained. As the airman lifted the board there was another explosion and one spent trigger device fell on the floor.

Neither sergeant laughed. They told the airman that he was dead, that he should have checked for a trap, and that he was a poor soldier. The NAAFI van arrived, we fell out but everyone was very careful on leaving their seat, opening doors and crossing the grass to get cups of tea.

After tea came the first fire arms lecture on the nine millimetre Sten gun. Sergeant Poore described it as a very cheaply produced automatic or single round weapon, capable of using any nine millimetre rimless ammunition. Quite a useful attribute if you ran out of ammo you could always use the enemy's. He also said it was probably made by the village blacksmith and if it went wrong to throw it away and draw another from stores. Joke! Although when we had chance to closely examine one, it did look as if it had been made by the village blacksmith.

He was describing the firing cycle and referring to diagrams and data written on the blackboard, when he came to the bottom of the board. He told an airman to clean it off. The airman picked the board duster off the table and the instant he applied it to the board there was another explosion.

Later in the week at the firing range we had the chance to fire the Sten. The magazine held twenty plus rounds, and when on automatic, one squeeze on the trigger emptied it in seconds. We were firing from the hip at a man-sized target at twenty-five yards. Several targets were actually sawn in half and collapsed as the constant stream of bullets totally smashed the vertical timber supports. We started out with eight sten guns and finished the session with only two still firing.

While at the range we also fired the .303 short Lee Enfield rifle and the Bren gun. The latter weapon was a highly engineered and very accurate semi-automatic gun using .303 ammunition. My scores at 100 yards, 500 yards and 1000 yards were pathetic.

It is only since taking up target archery when I had a simple test, that I learned I am left eye dominant, e.g. I sight through the bow string, foresight and gold with my left eye. If I used my right eye my arrows would go to the left of the target. No one in the RAF checked this or knew about it. Although I am right-handed I now shoot arrows left handed. How did we win the war?

After our day on the range we returned to the single Nissen hut and the training ground. We then spent time laying dummy mines and detecting them using metal detectors and also crawling over the ground and prodding it with our bayonets in the hope we didn't strike a buried solid object.

One of the lectures covered observation and Sergeant Plummer showed us the correct way to carry out observation. The demonstration was done at the training ground. We were sitting around on the grass, about twenty yards from a wall made of sandbags laid end to end and three sandbags high.

The sergeant wearing a tin hat, complete with camouflage net and vegetation disappeared over the other side of the sandbag wall. He was telling us that he was crawling over the ground towards the sandbags, so that he was not seen from the front, e.g. by us. Eventually we could see moving vegetation, followed by the camouflage net and part of the dome of his tin hat.

The dialogue continued 'Now I am at the observation point and I will observe.'

The tin helmet rose clear of the wall and the horizontal strip of his face containing his eyebrows and eyes appeared looking straight ahead. Vertical movement ceased. The tin hat and eyes rotated ninety degrees to the left, the motion was reversed and the eyes came ahead once more. Then the tin hat and eyes rotated ninety degrees to right, the motion reversed again and once more the eyes looked straight ahead. Finally the tin hat and the vegetation sank out of sight, to the words

'And that completes the observation.'

Captain Mainwaring could not have done it any better and when Sergeant Plummer came back over the wall he found thirty highly amused airmen rolling on the grass.

15

The Commanding Officers Weekly Inspection

The station commander's weekly inspection of all station personnel took place each Wednesday morning. The only exception was during the August block leave, three weeks, when the station was closed for flying and was more or less deserted by regular airmen for most of the period. National Service airmen never had that much leave.

The parade was held on the square which was at the centre of the domestic site. Three 'H' blocks faced the square across a service road and a strip of blast shelters on the north side. The south side was the same, except the line of blast shelters were broken in the middle by a space for the flagpole and its supporting cables.

The west side was flanked by one solitary 'H' block housing the WRAFs and referred to as the 'Waafery'. The service road ran in front of the block. The east side of the square was fronted by more blast shelters, behind which was the NAAFI club and the airmen's mess. Two short roads, at the east end, gave access onto the square from the north and south side service roads.

The north 'H' blocks were occupied by airmen attached to the squadrons – flying wing. On the south side, one block housed technical wing airmen and one administration wing airmen. The centre block was occupied by shift workers from both technical wing and administration wing. Behind these blocks were several single storey buildings occupied by an outstationed fighter control unit.

The uniform for the parade alternated each week between Number One dress and working dress. Prior to marching onto the square, each wing would form up in flights and squadrons on the roads around the square, where a very close inspection of individual turnout was made and any errors were rectified. Our wing commander was determined that we would have the best turn out.

Finally, the wings started to march onto the square, to music provided by the bands. Flying wing at the western end, in the centre technical wing and the administration wing at the eastern end, the WRAFs formed the rear flight of this Wing although not all were attached to it. The fighter plotting unit fell-in at the rear of the parade. The station bands – brass and pipe – also fell-in at the rear.

After, halting and turning to face the flag pole the wings were dressed, so that all ranks and flights were perfectly in line on both the x and y axes of the square. When this was complete the officer of the day handed the parade over to the station adjutant. At this point the CO would arrive, the RAF ensign would be broken on the flag mast as the adjutant gave the order 'General salute, Present arms'.

All airmen moved as one to bring their rifles to the present, the officers presented their swords and the bands played the general salute, which the CO returned with an arm salute. The next command was order arms and then the inspection began.

The station commanding officer – 'Ginger' –

inspected only one wing each week. He was followed around by an entourage which included the station adjutant, the wing commander, the squadron leader, the flight commander, the officer of the day, the station warrant officer and the squadron warrant officer. The last two carried pen and paper on which to record the names and numbers of any airman or airwoman directed to replace his/her uniform or was pulled up for some other shortcoming in their appearance.

I had ten weeks service still to do when the CO said that while my battledress was neat and pressed, it was so thread-bare I should replace it. The WOs descended, pens poised and were most disappointed when I said 'National Serviceman, less than twelve weeks service left, Sir'. But the SWO still took my name and number, possibly to prove I wasn't trying to pull a fast one.

After the inspection was completed, we would all march past, giving 'Ginger' a smart eyes right. We were marched off the square, halted and ordered to fall out and to return to our billets.

A billet inspection followed and if our wing had been inspected by the station CO there was a kit inspection and a billet inspection. The kit inspection consisted of a bed layout of specified items, as well as bedside locker and wardrobe layouts.

Finally when all the inspections were over we would go out and play at soldiers. Some airmen would be defending the station while others attempted to attack it.

The above activities started at 08.00 hours and ceased at about 12.30 hours, when all personnel proceeded to their respective messes for lunch. Wednesday afternoon was filled with almost everyone partaking in their chosen sport.

The Station Commander was nicknamed 'Ginger' by us (airmen). I cannot recollect his name. He was an ex flying type, all the WRAFs thought he was the answer to their prayers.

The RAF was running a recruiting campaign at this time with the slogan 'Join the RAF. Ginger's back'. I don't think the CO was that particular Ginger.

☆　　☆　　☆

Johnny IV

One of the many Johnnies was a regular airman, ex RAF apprentice, with apparent religious mania, obviously trying to work his ticket – release. If anyone he knew had an accident or fell ill, or was put on a fizzer – charge, Johnny would shower him or her with religious tracts threatening them with pestilence, plagues of locusts and lakes of fire and brimstone if they did not turn to God and repent. He may have saved a few souls but he was still in the RAF when I was demobbed.

16

Playing at Soldiers

Every Wednesday morning immediately following the station commanding officer's weekly parade and inspection all personnel not on essential duties, moved off to their allotted defence positions around the airfield.

My platoon's position was inside the bomb dump. The bomb dump is more or less what its title states, the munition stores. It was a series of sunken roads with many storage areas and blockhouses surrounded by earth banks and masonry walls. There were two ramped entrance roads on the north side of the dump.

I must confess I was a trifle nervous the first time I went into the dump, even though our position was on the perimeter road, on top of an earth bank and protected by a low brick wall. Behind us was a concrete blockhouse, with heavy steel doors and an overhead crane beam extending from the doors to the roadway.

The mind visualised large lumps of steel – cased high explosive just waiting for a shell or a bomb to land on it to trigger off an explosion, sending the block-house and all around into oblivion. Relief came later, when, after studying the notices displayed by the entrance roads and checking the coloured number painted on the blockhouse, we realised that the contents were only inflammable.

One sunny Wednesday morning in early summer we again marched off to our position in the bomb dump, complete with rifles and Ron and Johnny with the Bren gun, but no ammunition.

Several hundred more airmen were held in reserve with no fixed defence position and on this bright and still morning they were assigned to attack the station. The 'troops' left the parade ground in Bedford three ton trucks. I am now presuming that all servicemen will remember the notorious transmission/gearbox whine the Bedford three tonner made.

The first Bedford moved off and the gearbox noise drifted in the still morning air, followed at intervals by several more trucks. The transmission noise and the gear changes enabled their route to be followed.

The first change down was for the main gates, to be followed by either a left or right turn onto the main road. The noise increased, indicating a left turn had been made and the convoy of trucks was moving south behind us, between the married quarters and the sergeants' and officers' messes. The next change down was when they approached the cross roads at the top of the village.

Here they had the choice of three possible directions. The increasing vehicle noise soon showed they had turned left once more. The trucks were now passing on our righthand side about half a mile away.

As we looked east (forward) from our slightly elevated position behind the brickwall there was about twenty feet of open ground before a barbed wire fence, made up of three rolls of barbed wire stacked one on top of two, mixed up with several years growth of brambles. About 200 yards beyond the fence and over the recently cut grass were the tall, straggly and neglected remains of an old hawthorn hedge, fifteen to

84

thirty feet high, an ancient boundary between two fields. This hedge ran parallel to our position and on the left it suddenly stopped where it had been cleared when the airfield was created.

Behind the hedge and parallel to it there was one of the emergency crash exits. The crash exits allowed fire engines, crash tenders, ambulances etc to quickly leave the station to attend a crash incident, without having to make long detours outside the station. The airfield had several crash exits around its perimeter.

Meanwhile back at the ranch the trucks were changing down again and could now be seen approaching the crash exit junction with the county road. Surprise, surprise the trucks stopped and their passengers, about 450 men, climbed down and proceeded to form up into three flights.

They were then seen climbing over the crash exit fence and ambling down the opposite side of the old hedge until its very limited cover ran out. The attackers appeared to be non-plussed at their predicament. There was more than 500 yards of open grassland to the nearest building – Station Flight (Number Five) Hangar, so they all sat down and most lit up cigarettes to pass the time, while their leaders worked out a plan of campaign.

Ever since the attackers left the trucks the defenders in the bomb dump, nearly 200 men, had them under constant watch. We were told not to fire. Those defenders on the south and west sides of the bomb dump were withdrawn partly to reinforce the north and east sides and the remainder became reserves, hidden near the entrance roads.

The attacking force probably saw some of these movements and they eventually decided to attack us. They advanced across the hayfield, spreading out as they came, some firing blank ammunition. We had been ordered not to fire until they came within 100 yards.

Can you imagine how you fire at 100 yards, with no ammunition? Well with the then standard issue short Lee Enfield .303 rifle – mine had a date stamp on it of 1924 – firstly one pulled the bolt back, then one pushed the bolt forward, to push an imaginary round into the breech and finally one sighted the rifle on the target and squeezed the trigger, releasing the firing pin with a metallic click. To fire another theoretical round the process was repeated and so on and so on.

Ron and Johnny were Number one and Number Two on the Bren gun. Number One aimed and fired it, Number Two loaded it. Ron had pulled back the cocking handle and aimed the gun in the direction of the advancing hoard and shouted to Johnny 'Make a noise like a Bren gun.'

The attackers' advance came up against the brambles and the barbed wire. Like a wave coming onto a beach, they soon rolled back, before their leaders took them along the fence in a northerly direction. We were then ordered to move forward to the wire and follow them. Meanwhile defenders from our right were moving on the road below us towards the entrance.

A sergeant brandishing a revolver was leading one group of attackers. He was urging his men to move down the road into the dump. The road was less than twenty feet wide with steep banks on each side, the perfect defensive position. He chose to give his commands from the high ground adjacent to the road. He had nearly succeeded, when the attackers, who had been balked by the barbed wire, came behind him and one airman – who had ammunition – used the sergeant's shoulder as a rest for the muzzle of his rifle and fired off a blank round.

The sergeant fell to the ground clutching his right ear and screaming to all and sundry what he thought about the idiot who had rendered him deaf – or words to that effect. This apparent injury to one of the leaders led to a complete lack of interest in the battle and the more or less immediate cessation of hostilities for that day.

So we all went off to lunch. Some of us played cricket in the afternoon, whilst those who had actually fired their rifles spent the afternoon cleaning them.

☆　　☆　　☆

Oppy

Oppy was a corporal whose pastime was building and flying gliders, from small chuck gliders made from waste pieces of balsa wood, which littered the billet on wet weekends, to his pride and joy, a six foot wingspan aircraft, made of balsa and doped tissue paper.

In order to fly this giant Oppy needed another person to hold it for launch and to run behind Oppy who furiously pedalled his bike, with tow line attached, to obtain sufficient speed to lift the glider into the air. Some flights were unsuccessful and some resulted in damage.

On the more successful flight, Oppy would be seen riding out of the station chasing his glider across Norwich. At times he complained he had to offer reparation to the owner of the house or the garden the glider had crash landed onto or into.

17

Sailors and Sailing

All the services provided first class games and sports facilities and anyone could generally play his or her favourite game or participate in a chosen activity.

One station had its own golf cource. No doubt some past CO had been a fanatic. Since I was stationed in Norfolk a sailing club was one of our sporting facilities. It had one drawback – only officers were allowed to be helmsmen. This meant that any airman could only crew and to do that you put your name on a list and hoped to be asked to crew. I had my name on the list from Easter 1952 and it was still on it when I was demobbed in September 1953. I am still waiting to be asked.

The way round this problem was simple, three or four of us, who were interested in sailing, used to hire a sailing day boat from either Wroxham or Potter Heigham for a weekend. That was from Friday evening to Monday evening. A 'day boat' was an open cockpit boat which had no cabin. This was no problem, for with the boom supported on a crutch rest and the mainsail draped over the boom, four could sleep quite comfortably on the cockpit floor of a twenty-four footer. The sun always seemed to be shining in those days. I cannot remember it ever raining on any of our sailing weekends.

The sailing weekends needed a seventy-two hour pass to obtain a temporary ration card in order to eat because food was still rationed. The majority of pubs on the Broads gladly provided food in exchange for these pieces of paper as well as the necessary cash, so eating was no problem and drinking wasn't a problem either!

The first task on picking up the boat was to hoist sail, if there was a wind capable of taking us in the direction of the nearest pub. If not, the quant pole was used to 'quant' us there.

A quant pole – for the uninitiated – is a long wooden pole, about twenty feet long, with a large flat knob at the top and a wide piece of wood about a foot long fastened longtitudinally to the bottom to stop the quant sinking too far into the mud. It didn't always work. The person using the quant would stand near the bow, push the quant into the water, angled towards the stern and when it touched the bottom, push on the pole.

The boat would begin to move forward and the pusher would eventually be able to put his shoulder to the end of the pole and push whilst walking along the edge of the deck towards the stern. The tricky bit was when to decide to stop pushing and pull up the quant so that one did not walk off the stern holding onto a pole with no visible means of support.

When or if one has successfully pulled up the quant, one would walk back to the bow and repeat and repeat the operation until a bend in the river put the wind behind you or the pub turned up.

The first weekend we sailed from Wroxham to Horning, but on the way discovered Wroxham and Ranworth Broads. We consisted of one more or less expert sailor and three novices and had quanted from Wroxham into Wroxham Broad where we found some wind. The sails filled and we sailed majestically down the full length of the broad and managed to tack back to where we had started. We sailed up and down the broad several times before we were distracted by two girls in a rowing boat.

Our helmsman brought us alongside their boat and we chatted them up and offered them a sail with us, but they were not interested. The reason soon came roaring up: a very sleek motor boat, all polished wood, no stern, with the rear deck sloping gradually down into the water. It also contained two Yanks.

As we drifted away one of the girls passed the painter from the rowing boat across to the non-driving Yank, who made it off on a gleaming brass cleat on the sloping stern deck. He rejoined his companion who then proceeded to open the throttle wide. The motor boat's bow went up, while the stern went down and so did the bow of the rowing boat. The propeller wash also went up and over the bow of the rowing boat, which rapidly filled with water.

It was some time before the driver throttled back and two very wet girls struggled on to the motor boat. We could not resist pointing out, as we sailed past them, that our craft didn't have propellers and we were still dry.

We had decided to sail up and down the broad once again, but now there were many more sailing boats on the water. Some of them had the same symbol on their sails and they were in tight groups, with one crewman hanging over the side. Our course took us through one group and their shouts and remarks about our sailing were far from complimentary.

When we reached the far end of the broad we came about and proceeded to tack backwards and forwards to reach the other end, once more. Again we encountered these groups of small dinghies and again got shouted at as well as having several near misses. We were also threatened with physical violence, but no one came alongside.

It was soon apparent to us that most of these boats were sailing on a preset triangular course. The area in the middle of the triangle was clear water, so we sailed around in that area. On one beat we came close to the shore, where there was a very imposing pavilion, with concrete slipways into the water and a lot more boats on trailers scattered around the building. As we came nearer a voice boomed out from a loudspeaker telling *Plover II* to keep clear of the racing dinghies and to not interfere with the race.

Plover II was our boat, and the voice also described where the nearest exit from the broad to the river was and suggested we use it immediately. The pavilion was the club house of the Wroxham Sailing Club. We took the advice we were given and rejoined the river.

Once in the river the trees cut off the wind and the quant pole came into use again. Up to this point we hadn't had time to be bored but the river seemed endless and we were beginning to get thirsty as well as hungry. The sun was beginning to sink in the west and we had not found a pub yet.

The sun had set by the time we reached Ranworth Broad. The broad is not large, but there were about fifty sailing boats and motor cruisers already at anchor, most of them crewed by people on holiday. Also each boat had a small dinghy which the crews used to get ashore.

Nearly all the dinghies were tied up, ten deep around the small stone jetty in front of the pub, the only building in sight. We cautiously tied up against two of the dinghies and walked across them and several more to get to dry land and sustainance.

The pub was very crowded and warm. The place appeared to sway even before a drink. This turned out to be sea legs from the continued rocking motion of the boat. After being fed and well watered and turned out at closing time we found there was no direct route back to Plover II. It was now at anchor twenty-five feet away from the jetty.

After a noisy discussion, when suggestions such as swimming out to it were made, a kind gentleman who was moored nearby, came across in his dinghy and ferried us out to our boat. We then quanted it to the jetty, tied up and settled down for the night after a very full afternoon and evening.

Note – Ranworth Broad is now a nature reserve.

18

Nearly Real War Games

Another annual event was the yearly attack on the station by the Royal Air Force Regiment. The Regiment attacked other airfields in Norfolk while using our station as their base. They lived under canvas and as well as using the technical facilities available they also used the mess, the Naafi club for beer and recreation and the adjacent billets for their ablutions.

This cheek by jowl existence led to friendly contacts being made with members of the regiment. These contacts also provided the date of their attack on the station. The fifth column worked very well. It was amazing what a supply of charged batteries for tent lighting could do.

The date of the attack when compared with our shift roster showed that Ron and I were on duty that day and throughout the night. We decided that since most of the station would be involved in the exercise we would split the twenty-four hours into day, evening and night duties. Our chiefy agreed with the work plan. We would work together during the day and single the evening and night shifts. We tossed a coin and I won the evening shift.

D-day arrived, the day passed by and I went off for early tea. I relieved Ron at 17.30 hours and agreed to change over in the mess for supper at 21.00 hours, also the time when war would break out.

I was delayed in getting away at 21.00 hours because some erk wanted a vehicle battery and I left the acc-room at about 21.15 hours – war officially started at 21.00 hours, but we were not supposed to know.

As I was walking off the technical site, I was suddenly confronted by a khaki-drill clad, tin-helmeted one-armed figure brandishing a revolver, who jumped out of a shrubbery and asked me 'If I knew there was a war on and why I hadn't saluted an officer'.

I replied, that I was on duty and therefore not part of the war, and since he was not displaying any badges of rank how was I supposed to know he was an officer?

Note – there was only one one-armed officer on the station and he was a squadron leader in charge of the stores, also only officers and senior ncos were allowed revolvers. I didn't tell him I knew who he was, it might have spoiled his war. He told me to get on my way. We exchanged salutes; he went off into the sunset and I carried on to the mess.

After supper I walked over to the billet, crossing the parade ground on the way. This vast area of tarmac was rapidly filling up with vehicles. Rows of Jeeps and Land Rovers, thirty-hundred weight and three ton Bedfords, buses, bloodwagons (ambulances), petrol bowsers, cranes, staff cars, fire tenders, nearly every vehicle on the station.

On entering the billet there was a mass of activity. People in KD with blackened faces and carrying rifles turned out to be GCA radar staff formed into a search and attack group. Their job was to go out and find the enemy. They went out into the night and we who were left in the billet went to bed.

The start of the 'war' was a very spasmodic affair, only an occasional rifle shot was heard. It was hardly enough to keep one awake. But about 01.00 hours all hell broke loose with more rifle fire, loud explosions and blinding flashes of light around the main gate, the guardroom and station headquarters. This activity carried on for the next hour before dying down.

Meanwhile we, the non-combatants watching from our billet windows, saw shadowy figures moving among the vehicles parked on the square. In the light of thunderflashes and flares it was possible to see one vehicle after another settle down on flat tyres. Infiltrating attackers let the air out of every tyre of all the parked vehicles.

Shortly after 02.00 hours an announcement over the tannoy said the attacks had been repulsed and the war was over. We, the station, had won the 'war'. Officers and NCOs would command everyone to cease firing.

This broadcast started world war three. The noise of discharging rifles was greater than when the major attack took place and took more than half an hour to quieten down.

As peace descended the search and attack group returned to the billet. From my bed I could see out into part of the entrance hall. Eric came into view and Paddy's voice rang out 'Halt or I fire.' Eric replied 'Balls!' and bent over. There followed an almighty explosion. Eric shot upright, hand on bottom, shouting 'You've shot me you bastard' or words to that effect. The explosion was one .303 blank round fired in a brick and concrete building.

Eric was still hopping around crying 'I've been shot' when a new voice was heard. The station warrant officer was ordering two unseen airmen to form an escort. He was putting Paddy under arrest for disobeying a lawful order to cease firing.

Paddy got off that charge because the search and

attack group were off the station at the time the order was broadcast. But he got fourteen days jankers for shooting Eric. Poor Eric did suffer. The cardboard wad from the blank round, which was fired about three feet from his bum, had penetrated four layers of clothing before embedding itself in his tender behind.

The search and attack group had gone across the airfield in two to three feet of ground mist. They crawled on hands and knees using the fog as cover, occasionally rising to look above it, to see where they were going. On more than one occasion as they stuck their heads out of the fog, they were looking at RAF Regiment attackers going in the opposite direction. But each dropped down into the mist and passed on.

The following morning Ron came off duty to say that he had been held prisoner by Search And Destroy parties from the Regiment, they had tea together. But every building was theoretically destroyed by the dummy bombs placed against them.

It took two days to clear the disabled vehicles from the square and several more before Eric's bottom had healed.

An Airman – Charlie II

Charlie II was a regular airman and an SAC – radar mechanic. When he wanted a shave he would plug his electric razor into one of the eight pendant light fittings, sit on his pit and shave away.

His razor caused interference on the radio and he would pick up one of the chairs, hold it in front of him with the legs pointing away from him. By varying the pressure of the razor against his face he could change the pitch and state of the interference.

He would then play out the role of a bomber rear gunner. The radio noise became the roar of the bomber's engines as he yelled 'Bandits two o-clock, corkscrew right, corkscrew left or dive' to his imaginary pilot. In between the shouted instruction he would fire his chair leg machine guns 'ratatatatat——'.

We had at least one performance a week, usually on 'bull night' so he was ready for the CO's parade the next day.

Charlie liked to ride his bike around on the billet flat roof and on one occasion someone bet him he wouldn't ride off the roof, which was like a red rag to a bull. Charlie went to far end of the roof and pedalled like mad along it and off into space – crash, Charlie ended up with a bent ankle and a bent bike.

An Officer and a Gentleman

One morning Andy, from 245 Squadron, stuck his head in the acc-room door and asked if we had seen the Meteor which had just parked between the hangers.

We moved into the office and saw through the window an immaculate Mark Eight, painted olive green and polished like perfectly bulled boot toe caps.

A station flight ground crew were already in attendance and the pilot was climbing down with his tunic jacket over his arm. When he got to the ground he put the jacket on the wing and took off his flying suit, put on and buttoned up his jacket. I cannot remember his rank – he was either a group captain or an air vice marshal.

He pulled a comb from his breast pocket and combed his hair, looking at his reflection in his aircraft's paint job. He rolled up his flying suit climbed back up to the cockpit and put it on the seat. He next reached behind the seat for his peaked cap, stowed in one of the ammunition boxes.

Once more he climbed down to the ground and like a magician took a yellow duster out of his cap, polished its peak, placed the cap on his head, checking its position in the paint mirror. Then he polished his shoes with the duster, using the Meteor's bottom step as a footrest.

Finally, he tossed the duster up into the cockpit, spoke to the ground crew and walked over to the waiting Humber staff car which took him off to group headquarters.

19

With Full Military Honours

A recurring function for the guard of honour was to provide the escort at the full military honours funerals of officers and airmen when these took place locally. The services were held at the village parish church. Luckily I was not tall enough for the firing party and I was saved from the additional chore of cleaning my rifle after firing the volleys by the graveside.

The station had two bands– one brass band and one pipe band. I now have a built in dislike of pipe bands. The dislike arose from the escort part of the funeral ceremonial.

The funeral consisted of four definite parts. The first came when the pipe band, guard of honour and firing party assembled on the road adjacent to the square, marched onto the square for a detailed inspection, before quick marching to the beat of a single side drum to the mortuary, adjacent to the station sick quarters.

The hearse was waiting. It was a 'Karrier Bantam' – a small flat-bed truck. The truck bed was covered with artifical grass on which was a small black platform. Along the truck sides were short white posts with a blancoed white rope threaded through them.

The parade formed up with the guard of honour and the firing party at the head, then the pipe band and the hearse. The bearer party, six members of the guard of honour, all the same height would then carry the coffin from the mortuary, place it on the platform on the hearse and then stand three on each side.

The officer of the day and the SWO would drape the RAF Ensign over the coffin. If the funeral was for an officer, his cap, gloves and sword were also placed on the coffin: for an airman his beret would be on the coffin.

When all the preparations were complete the command 'by the left slow march' was given and the column moved off to the pipes playing a lament. I still cringe when I hear bagpipes playing a lament. It was about half a mile from sick quarters to the station headquarters and we slow marched all the way with the blurrn blurrn moaning sound of the pipes' drones.

Meanwhile at HQ the brass band was waiting together with the station CO, relatives and mourners. As we turned onto the road to HQ several cars would be waiting to join on behind the hearse. The parade halted behind the brass band, the lament stopped and the relatives and official mourners were shown into cars.

Anyone from the station who wished to attend would fall in behind the cars. Usually fifty to a hundred airmen and airwomen came to show their respect. Many were saying goodbye to a friend.

Eventually we would receive the order 'attention' followed by 'right turn' and then 'by the left slow march' and once more we moved off to the pipes still playing a lament.

The brass band led the way forward through the main gates, the drum major signalled 'left wheel' with his mace as he moved onto the road and as the last rank of the brass band completed the turn the order 'Breaking into quick time – quick march' was given, the pipes ceased immediately and the brass band struck up with a quick march – usually 'This is the army Mr Jones'.

The march took the procession past the NAAFI shop on the left, airmen's married quarters on the right. Next the sergeants' mess followed by the officers' mess on the left, with the officers' married quarters on the right as we climbed the hill to the crossroads at the top of the village.

The village sign was a cat on a barrel and as the brass band passed it the order 'breaking into slow time – slow march' ended the quick march and the lament played until the column halted at the small church.

The bearer party carried the coffin into church for the service and the relatives and mourners also went in, but the bands and the guard of honour remained outside on the road, whatever the weather. After the service the interment took place in the churchyard. The firing party fired their volleys over the grave, the mourners returned to the cars and departed.

Finally, the bands, the guard of honour and the firing party, with the bearers back in the ranks marched back to the station to the single drum beating time. The route back was shortened by going through the sergeants' mess entrance and then onto the square for dismissal and return to normal duties.

Near Disasters

The acc-room was located in the workshops attached to Number three hangar with a radio section in the adjacent workshop. A radio set was always tuned to the 'mayday' frequency. When any pilot called out 'may-day mayday – – ' it was round the station grapevine in a flash.

One such call came from a Meteor pilot reporting thuds and bangs under the aircraft as he took off. Apart from the noises the aircraft was flying normally. From tyre debris found on the runway, it was deduced that a main wheel tyre had shed its tread and the noises were caused by pieces of the rubber-graphite mixture hitting the aircraft.

The Meteor flew very low and slow over the control tower with its undercarriage down while several officer types with binoculars confirmed one tyre minus tread. The pilot then flew round in continuous circles to use up fuel and most of the rest of the station went off to tea.

The aircraft was still going round in circles after tea and small groups of onlookers began to appear by the hangars. Fire engines, crash tenders, an ambulance and the Coles crane were now parked on the grass alongside the runway.

The pilot made several more circuits and a couple of low passes over the control tower before joining the landing pattern. The airfield had a hump in it and as the aircraft descended for an east to west landing it disappeared from view below the hump. It seemed like ages before the Meteor appeared over the hill, after making a normal landing on all three wheels, being chased by the crash tenders, the ambulance and the crane.

The pilot opened the canopy, stopped and very quickly jumped down from the aircraft leaving the crash crews to tow it back to the hangar.

On another occasion, one of the RAAF Vampire pilots called up to say he had no hydraulics. The same procedure as before, low passes over the control tower, showed nothing except the wheels would not lower.

While the Aussie pilot formated with and flew in circles with a mate, the crash tenders, fire engines, the ambulance and the crane took up their positions, on the runway this time.

The pair of aircraft made several trial passes down the length of runway. Disappearing as they descended then both appearing still airborne. Finally only one Vampire climbed up above the airfield. The wait began again. No smoke so it hadn't crashed. Then it came over the hump bouncing along on the grass, being chased by the crane and the ambulance.

As the aircraft still slithered to a halt the medics were off the ambulance, jumping up onto the wings and opening the canopy. It seemed like ages before they and the pilot climbed down and got into the ambulance, which then tore off to sick quarters. The pilot was discharged later with no damage or ill effects from his ordeal.

The Vampire was lifted onto a recovery platform and repaired in time to go onto the USA with the rest of the wing.

20

Weather

The summers in East Anglia, from memory, were long and hot, while the winters were very cold, with extended periods of very strong and bitterly cold easterly winds, coupled at times with heavy snow falls.

The twenty-four hours on and twenty-four hours off shift working pattern led to alternate summer afternoons being spent on the beach at Yarmouth or in a swimming pool in Norwich, depending on the prevailing cash situation for petrol in the motor bike tank or admission to the pool. In the winter the afternoons were either spent in bed or visiting the many museums and art galleries in Norwich. On a conducted tour of the Cathedral, Ron and I climbed up the inside of the spire. The view from the top was fantastic, in spite of the supporting steelwork.

On Saturday 31 January 1953 I was duty electrician. It was a wet and windy day. The wind was initially from the west and through the day the wind speed increased and the direction moved through north-west to north. During the afternoon a tannoy call wanted the duty electrician to report to air traffic.

I duly arrived at the tower and was told the GCA Unit was closing down and moving under cover, but they were having difficulty lowering some of the scanning aerials because of the wind speed. It was already difficult to stand upright in the wind.

I drove out to the GCA Unit, halfway down the main runway. The GCA duty crew with the help of others and myself eventually dropped and secured the aerials. I disconnected the generators and a convoy of two American Diamond Tee trucks, one towing the long GCA caravan, followed by me in a thirty-hundredweight Bedford made for the shelter of the hangars. I had several more calls during the night relating to failed security lights, but prevailed on the guardroom to leave them until daylight when the windspeed should have dropped sufficiently to allow easy movement.

The high winds were caused by an intense low pressure system moving between Iceland and Scotland, and then passing over Norway. The system set up a surge tide which passed down the North Sea through the night. Unfortunately, this surge coincided with the high tide also moving down the North Sea. The resulting abnormally high water caused severe flooding from north Lincolnshire to north Kent and across to Holland. As well as causing considerable damage to sea defences in England and Holland, many lives were also lost.

Flying was abandoned and all normal duties ceased. The tannoy informed all personnel of their future duties for the following days. Two days later the electrical section, ground equipment section, GCA unit and air traffic receivers staffs arrived by truck in Great Yarmouth, to fill the breaks in the flood banks on the south side of Breydon Water, a long and wide broad to the north of Yarmouth, which is part of the river Waveney.

Large areas of the town had been flooded. The effects were soon apparent as we drove along streets of terraced houses, where carpets and furniture had been put up onto garden walls to try and dry them.

We arrived in a farmyard by the embankment carrying the railway to the swing-bridge over the Waveney and into Vauxhall station. An overbridge in the embankment had been blocked with debris to stop the flood-water flowing into the town at times of high tide.

The view from the top of the embankment, looking north and west to east, was of an immense lake, stretching from the foot of the embankment as far as the eye could see. Trees, high hedges, farm building, houses and decaying windmills completely surrounded by water, greyish brown water turning grey in the distance.

The nearest building was a small bungalow, about 300 yards away, standing in five or six feet of water. One fatality occurred here caused by the sudden inrush of flood water. The broken flood banks were a quarter of a mile beyond the bungalow.

Sandbags were filled on Yarmouth beach and brought to the farmyard by lorries. Our task was to unload them, carry them up and over the embankment and load them into DKWS – DUCKS – American amphibious trucks – and a 'Terrapin' on loan from The Yorkshire Ouse River Board.

The terrapin looked like a large waste skip with four large tractor wheels on an arc on each side. All the wheels were driven, it floated and the wheel arrangement allowed it to easily climb any obstacle in its path. But like the DUCKS its speed in deep water was about as fast as a person walking. At low tide all the amphibians' wheels were in contact with the ground and speed increased but as the tide rose and they started to float, speed fell.

106

The slow passage of sandbags to the breached flood banks led to a large build up of sandbags on the 'dry' side of the embankment, that is when it wasn't snowing or raining. Also there were long periods of inactivity and it was cold.

The blocked bridge made a convenient shelter and whilst under its protection it became obvious that a re-arrangement of the debris keeping back the tides would allow the unloading and reloading to be done without having to climb up and down the embankment.

The NCOs present agreed and we filled in a ditch in front of the bridge. This allowed the trucks to get in and out more easily. Spare sandbags quickly formed an unloading bay for two trucks and finally a loading dock for two amphibians was built on the flooded side. All our work was done in the dry and the unloading and reloading was more or less a horizontal transfer.

The re-arrangement led to a great saving in manpower and many of us were moved further up the coast to Sea Palling. Here the surge tide had made a huge gap in the low sand and marram grass hills, which appeared to be the only defence against the sea.

The road into the village ended at about the centre of the gap, where there had been two pubs. The pub on the right was still standing but only the chimney stack and the pub sign remained of the one which had been on the left. The village street was several feet deep in sand, dropped by the water as it rushed inland. Sea Palling also suffered casualties.

Our task, with the help of the Royal Canadian Air Force was to build a sea wall of sand bags across the gap, nearly one hundred yards long and fifteen yards wide at the base. A county council bulldozer driver dug a wide trench along the beach and twenty sand bags were laid end to end across it. Another line was laid beside the first and the process repeated right across the whole gap.

While the base layer was being completed, a second layer of sandbags was laid on top of and at right angles to the first layer. Then a third layer was laid like the first. Even layers in one direction and odd layers at right angles to them. The seaward edge of each succeeding layer of sand bags was set back from the previous layer. The finished effect was like a long curved stairway fifteen feet high.

From time to time the bulldozer pushed sand up and over the rising sand bag barrier to give strength and support behind it. The final task was to dig out the village street.

The Sea Palling wall completed, we moved up the coast again to the end of a farm track where a concrete sea wall had collapsed at many places and seawater had rushed miles inland. A large ship was high and dry about half a mile further up the beach.

The sea wall had a massive concrete base of horizontal inverted vees pointing at the sea, with four deep concrete steps leading up to a curved wall made from concrete filled sacks dropped onto steel reinforcing bars. The back of the wall was a sand bank varying between ten and thirty yards wide but only slightly higher than the seawall. The farmland behind was lower than the concrete base to the wall. Parts of the top section of the sea wall had collapsed although the base was still sound.

Successive tides had penetrated the small gaps between the sacks and leeched the sand out from behind. Time had also rusted away the steel reinforcing bars. The surge tide was probably the last straw, pushing over the already weak wall into the voids behind and rapidly washing out more sand before finally breaking through to the lower land behind.

The first task was to move the concrete debris to one side, then to build a sand bag wall similar to the one at Sea Palling and backfill. The backfill here was the broken sea wall and sand pushed up by bulldozers from the beach.

All this work took place in February and early March. The weather varied from warm sunshine to bitterly cold winds straight off the sea, mixed in with periods of rain and snow. A pair of knitted woollen, standard issue, gloves wore out in two days of filling and carrying sand bags – industrial gloves were unheard of. Working dress was worn under overalls, with a British warm – a leather body warmer – on top. The head and ears were kept warm by a cap comforter – a knitted woollen sleeve sewn up at one end. Issued wellingtons and seaboot socks kept the feet warm.

Food provided by the RAF was usually cold, doorstep thick corned beef or cheese sandwiches together with a cold hardboiled egg plus lukewarm tea out of the urns we took out each day. Food provided by the army catering corp was cooked in field kitchens on site – meat and two veg plus pudding all hot – hot tea was available all day. At Sea Palling a Red Shield mobile canteen provided hot tea, sandwiches and cake at no cost. I always give freely to Salvation Army collections in memory of their Red Shield Canteens.

Guard Duty

I only took part in this chore during the final six months of my national service, apart from RAF Padgate.

The guard roster was drawn up by the SWO's office and any airman rank made up the general guard – eighteen men, others included NCOs and an officer acting as guard commander.

The period of guard duty was eighteen hours (weekdays) starting at 12.00 hours until 06.00 hours the following day and a ceremony at 18.00 hours on that day. The period of guard duty was twenty-four hours on Saturday and Sunday. The eighteen airmen were split into three units of six and each unit was divided into three pairs. Each pair stayed together throughout the guard.

The dress for guard duty was best blue, greatcoat, webbing belt and rifle. The ceremonial started, after tea, at 17.45 hours with fall in and inspection by the guard commander and the senior NCO in front of the guardroom. While this was going on the 'old' guard were being similarly treated at the other side of the flagpole in front of station HQ.

The two guards were finally formed up facing each other across the flagpole at station head quarters. The old guard commander then passed to the new guard commander the responsibility for the security of the station, the buildings, the equipment and the personnel on behalf of Her Majesty, including one prisoner in the custody of the RAF Police.

The ceremony finished, the old guard marched away and we fell out and went into the guardroom. The guardroom contained the RAF Police offices, several cells, an enclosed exercise yard, a firestation – complete with fire tender, and the guards room, plus the usual offices.

The guards room had several beds and some decrepit easy chairs, a stove and a table and six chairs. The guards tasks were divided to cover three activities.

110

1. to assist the snoop on gate duty passing personnel and civilians 'on and off' of the station.
2. & 3. to patrol the station and check security of all buildings and installations.

Number one was the cushy job inside while two and three could be cold and wet outside. I was in two with third shift. Each pair did a stint of the two hours on guard and four hours off in the guard room.

The first pairs took up their duties immediately, and four of us were told off to go to the mess and draw the guards' rations. Armed with a chit and a two gallon galvanised bucket we went down to the mess.

The rations consisted of one and a half pounds of tea, six pounds of sugar and nine tins of condensed milk. Supper was eaten in the mess between 21.00 hours and midnight. Half a pound of tea was put into the washed out bucket and the bucket filled with boiling water. Two of the ration party carried it back to the guardroom, while the other two carried the sugar and milk.

The bucket was placed on the stove and two pounds of sugar, together with three tins of condensed milk were poured into the tea and the liquid was stirred for a while to dissolve the sugar. Any member of the guard wanting a cup of tea just dipped his mug into the brew. It was very sweet and sticky, this was probably caused by the heat from the stove caramelising the milk. The primitive tea urn was twice recharged during the night.

RAF police directed the guards' security routes and patrol areas. It was impossible not to do the security checks and patrol because you nearly always met a snoop or snoop dog handler at least once during your two hour stints.

111

At the changing of the guard a prisoner in the custody of the RAF police was mentioned. He was a headcase from Merseyside, who considered we wanted our heads examining. All he did was keep his cell clean, his food was brought to him and he made tea for the snoops. His cell door was only locked from 24.00 hours to 06.00 hours. It transpired that the prisoner had spent most of his National Service in a cell. Whenever the chance came he was off over the wall, flogged his kit, had a few weeks 'freedom' before he was picked up and returned to the RAF. He boasted he had escaped seven times in fourteen months.

21

Tinker, Tailor, Accountant – Airman

In early 1953 the nightfighter squadrons flew away, thank goodness. The Vampire NF 10's turbine emitted a high pitched whine when the aircraft was taxi-ing. The noise made it difficult to sleep when they were flying. Their departure also removed the need for our shift working.

Several electrical mechanics moved out of the accroom into the electrical section workshop. Our first task was to complete the static Meteor test rig. The rig allowed most of the electrical components on a Meteor to be repaired, adjusted and tested off the aircraft, that is flown on the ground.

The second task was to establish a tested stock holding of two sets of Meteor electrical components.

The need for the test facility and the stores soon became obvious. The Air Ministry in its wisdom had decided that all us expensively trained airmen should earn our keep and carry out the major overhauls on the Gloster Meteor Mark 8 fighters. The more likely reason was that with so many Meteors in service Glosters could not do all the work.

The work force also included the 'C' flights from the day fighter squadrons still on the station. Finally more than 200 airmen of differing trades, with a lot of equipment, were brought together in Number Two hangar and the first aircraft from 245 squadron was towed in.

Airframe riggers jacked it off its wheels onto castored stands and scaffolding and started to remove the ailerons, flaps, rudder and elevator control surfaces, also the cockpit canopy. Ground equipment mechanics removed the wheels. Engine fitters and mechanics removed the jet engines. Armourers took out the twenty millimetre canons and the ejector seat.

Radar and radio mechanics removed radar and radio sets. Electrical mechanics removed starter panels, generators, control relays, gun and rocket firing mechanisms, bomb release switches, landing lights and so on. Instrument mechanics took off the bits which interested them.

The aircraft soon became an aluminum skeleton, containing only control cables, fuel tanks and fixed wiring. As another aircraft was brought in to the hangar the first was moved to one side and the stripping process started again. Eventually three rows of Meteors were moving down the hangar in various stages of dis-assembly and re-assembly.

As the weeks progressed, the original Meteor was rebuilt with many of it's original components, although some new spares were used from the stores stockpile. In theory the stock-holding was always two aircraft sets.

The aircraft was finally towed out of the hangar and filled with fuel. The engines were run up and tests were made to check engine jet pipe temperatures and synchronise power output.

The next day a pilot examined the aircraft externally and checked the operation of the control surfaces. Finally he removed the red and white sleeve from the pitot head tube and climbed into the cockpit. Before he sat down he removed the safety clip and disc on top of the ejector seat. The attendant mechanic helped the pilot fasten the parachute/seat harness straps before he climbed down from the side of the cockpit.

The pilot started each engine in turn, signalled to the mechanic who switched the electrical supply from ground to flight and un-plugged and removed the trolley acc ground supply trailer. During this procedure many of the airmen from Number Two hangar were stood around the open hangar doors watching.

The forward view from this point was in the front of the aircraft out along the taxi track to the main runway threshold about five hundred yards away. The pilot seemed to spend a very long time before he slid the cockpit canopy closed and signalled to the ground mechanic to remove the wheel chocks. The mechanic removed the chocks and moved clear of the port wing tip.

The engine noise increased, the pilot released the brakes and the aircraft began to move forward. After fifty yards he turned left onto the taxi track where he was held for several minutes by four Meteors coming in to land. Finally he turned right and stopped pointing down the runway.

Again the cockpit checks seem to take ages before the exhaust roar from the engines rose to a miniature thunderstorm. The Meteor's nose lifted several inches as the pilot released the brakes. It began to move instantly, the speed increasing every second as if the aircraft wanted to hurry into its own environment. After four to five hundred yards the nose wheel lifted off the tarmac, the mainwheels stayed on the ground for another five hundred yards before clear air appeared beneath them.

The aircraft climbed slowly, its wheels retracting as

it gained more height. At this point someone in the crowd of watchers said 'It flies, it bloody well flies.'

This statement broke the tension that had built up in the onlookers, someone else started clapping and we ended up applauding ourselves for completing the job we had been trained for.

22

The 78th Fighter Wing Royal Australian Air Force

Ceremonial parades were held for various reasons such as visiting royalty and diplomats, overseas air forces, AOC's visits, state occasions, military funerals etc. The drill movements involved were an extension of those learned during the basic training square bashing. The major part of the drill associated with these parades was performed by the guard of honour, of which I was a co-opted member.

The unfortunate members of the guard of honour had the additional bull of maintaining the Number One dress uniform and boots in an immaculate state, as well as providing white blanco to maintain the white webbing for these special parades.

1953 was the year of the Queen's Coronation and many extra parades were held in the weeks leading up to Coronation Day.

One of these parades was to provide the guard of honour for the Australian High Commissioner's visit to the 78th Fighter Wing of the Royal Australian Air Force. The Wing was on a Cook's Tour of the world and just happened to be on station for several weeks either side of Coronation Day.

The Australians were a self-contained unit, in that they had all the necessary support staff for servicing and maintaining their Vampire fighter aircraft as well as the inner man. But they did very little, if anything, in the way of bull. An RAAF airman's best blue (navy) uniform was in no way different to an officer's uniform, apart from the badges of rank. They wore peaked caps and they had no brass buttons, buckles or badges to polish, these were all black plastic, or brass painted black.

The working dress was a pair of overalls topped off with the peaked cap. The overalls varied in colour from dark blue to practically white dependant on age and the older ones sported many patches.

The airmen were paid nearly ten times our pay – £20 against £2. Although we were jealous, the Aussies were very generous. If an Aussie was drinking you drank as well and usually both of you ended up under the table.

The fighter wing was due for a visit from the Australian High Commissioner and the guard of honour commenced rehearsals. During one of the drill parades it was announced that since the Aussies wore peaked caps the parade would look better if all involved personnel also wore peak caps. Therefore all other rank members of the guard of honour were told to get peak caps.

This order immediately created a major problem. National Service airmen with less than twelve weeks service left to do were exempt from having to obtain replacement clothing. I was one of about twenty such airmen on parade. The SWO went through his usual ten shades of pink to red when this was pointed out to him.

The officer in charge of the parade offered a compromise which was acceptable to him. For the practice parades berets would be worn, but everyone would have his peak cap the day before the actual parade. National Service airmen (short time) would draw caps from the stores, again the day before, but on loan and return them into store after the parade.

Honour was satisfied until we went to draw the caps from stores. The warrant officer in charge of stores wanted the caps returned in perfect condition, as new, without hair oil stains on the hat band. This apparent impasse ended up with the issue of several sheets of tissue paper with which to line the interior of the caps to avoid soiling them.

The day dawned, it was grey and quite windy. At the appropriate time the members of the guard of honour and the brass band congregated on the road next to the square, were told to get fell in and were marched onto the square, halted, right turned and ordered into open order for inspection by the SWO. His inspection covered every aspect of every airman from head to toe, with many comments and many minor adjustments to clothing and equipment.

Meanwhile the Australian airmen had also fallen in and joined us on the square. When the inspections were complete, the order 'close order march' closed the ranks. All the parade was given the order 'right turn, by the left quick march' and we moved off behind the band, followed by three flights of Australians. We marched off the domestic site and halted between Number two and three hangars. This area of concrete was larger than the parade ground.

We formed two sides of a square. The guard of honour's back to the doors of Number Three hangar and the Australian flights on our left, facing the control tower. The closed doors of Number Two hangar and the control tower and the airfield formed the other sides of the square. Once again we were formed up in open order and again inspected, while the Aussies had a smoke.

119

As we waited for the aircraft carrying the Australian High Commissioner to arrive the wind blew the odd leaf or piece of paper across the concrete. Some airmen indulged in small talk, others attempted to see down their rifle muzzles or just gazed into the distance. The officers stood chatting together.

Eventually the drone of an aircraft filled the air, a Viking flew overhead and joined the landing circuit pattern. We were brought to attention, sloped arms, moved into open order, ordered arms and stood at ease.

After several minutes the Viking appeared and taxied to a halt in the space in front of Number Two hangar doors. After a final burst of engine noise the propellers windmilled to a halt. The steps were pushed forward by station flight ground crew dressed in immaculate white overalls. The aircraft door opened and for some considerable time nothing happened.

Then a small man in a city suit and homburg hat appeared at the doorway, and as he moved forward onto the steps. we received the order 'Attention' followed by 'slope arms'. The next command was 'general salute – present arms'.

The drill movements needed to present arms were:

1. lift the rifle off shoulder and carry to front of body.
2. keeping the rifle vertical, lower it down front of the body so that the sight and muzzle end up about eye height.
3. pull rifle into body and at the same time lift and place right foot behind left foot, stamping it on the ground.

While this drill movement was going on the officer of

the day moved his sword in a similar salute and the brass band was playing the RAF General Salute. But back at the guard of honour with the second drill movement all hell let loose, nearly all the rifle foresights caught the brims of the peaked caps, dislodging many and leaving some awry. Mine was amongst those on the ground and the wind was already beginning to blow some of the tissue paper temporary linings into the air.

Meanwhile on top of the steps the high commissioner did not bat an eyelid, he simply removed his hat and held it against his chest until the salute was finished. He then descended the steps and was introduced to the Australian CO, the station CO and several other officers and senior NCOs. During this time we sloped arms and then ordered arms in a sea of caps and wind blown tissue paper.

After the introductions the commissioner moved across to inspect the guard of honour accompanied by the staff mentioned above. As he moved along the ranks caps were kicked out the way and he would stop occasionally to speak to an airman. He stopped to have a word with an airman in front of me whose cap was hanging over his eyes, he lifted the cap back onto the airman's head, said a few words, had a chuckle, and moved on. After inspecting us the party moved over to the waiting Australian airmen.

We were then ordered to ground arms (place our rifles on the ground), then stand at ease, stand easy, and fall out to recover caps. It took several minutes before everyone found a cap which fitted and most of the tissue paper had blown away. After falling in once more we marched past the high commissioner and then back to the parade ground to be dismissed and some of us returned rather battered peaked caps to stores.

The Aussies said the parade was fair dinkum as well as being a load of bull and a good laugh. They bought the beer that night.

23

The Norwich Coronation Parade

The coronation of Her Majesty the Queen led to many additional duties. On the day before the coronation, aircraft from the station's squadrons flew to RAF Odiham in Hampshire to take part in the London flypast and ground crews went overland to service them. Also on the evening before, it was planned to have a large parade through Norwich.

The parade was made up of contingents from all three armed services, together with the public services and many youth organisations.

The parade route covered nearly three miles and it was decreed that the involved Horsham airmen, over 600 including the guard of honour, would get fit by marching around the perimeter track. Also because of the route length it would be sensible to 'change shoulders on the march.' This drill exercise consisted of a series of movements to transfer the rifle from one shoulder to the other. It was intended to give the supporting arm a rest and restore blood circulation.

After watching our many attempts to get it together the officers and NCOs decided it would look better for us to march with the rifles on the left shoulder for the entire march.

Anyone who remembers coronation day or has seen films of the occasion will be aware that it rained very hard most of the day. The previous evening was no exception. It was raining as we were bussed to the Nelson barracks, in Norwich. It rained as we fell in, as we marched, as we fell out and it was still raining when we arrived back at the station some time later.

The march was led by a Royal Navy band and a contingent of matelots, followed by an army band and several hundred men from a Royal Artillery anti-aircraft regiment with another band in the middle. The Royal Air Force came next with our brass band leading and the pipe band in the middle, the numbers were doubled by airmen from RAF Coltishall and their two bands.

The civilian section was headed by the police force, followed by the fire brigades, ambulance officers, nurses, naval cadet force, army cadet force, air training corps, scouts and guides, St John Ambulance, the Red Cross, WRVS and so on.

The parade marched out of the barracks along Riverside Road, right wheeled into Prince of Wales Road in the rain. But it had not deterred the people of Norwich from turning out and cheering us on our way. The children shouted and waved union jacks, while their parents shouted and applauded. Some people had the advantage of keeping dry by using first floor office windows as vantage points.

Through it all the rain still poured down. It ran down the length of the rifle into the palm of your hand, it trickled through your fingers only to fall again onto your left trouser leg and finally into your left boot. The march went on.

I was in the left hand file and when the road went slightly left I could see that side of the procession for some distance ahead. The army nearest our band was in step with us, those adjacent to their band were a

124

whole step out and the poor blokes in the middle were anywhere.

The parade continued up Prince of Wales Road and along Castle Meadow, where we had been told the saluting base would be. We had nearly completed the circuit of Castle Meadow when the order 'eyes left' came over above the music and cheering. As I moved my head to the left I glanced ahead to find the saluting base. All I saw in that glance was an empty footpath backed by a red brick wall. At this point the whole flight started to lose step, the road surface was rippled and ridged, by the time we had sorted ourselves out, the order 'eyes front' rang out. The saluting base, complete with canopy and assembled dignitaries, was in the carpark behind the red brick wall, about twelve feet above the road.

At the junction with Red Lion Street we right-wheeled past an undeveloped bombed-site into the Haymarket and carried on through the open market and the procession rightwheeled once more into London Street. Jarrold's bookshop was on the corner of London street and the fall pipes must have been blocked since a column of water was falling from the roof gutter into the roadway.

The cheering crowds and the line of march made it impossible for the left hand column to avoid marching through it. Apart from already having a wet head, hands, trouser legs and a left boot full of water, the walk through the deluge ensured that the rest of the body was soaked as well.

The sodden march went on into the Plain and back to Castle Meadow – people still cheered – down Prince of Wales Road, left into Tombland and finally to the barracks for dismissal and back to camp for a hot shower and dry out.

125

Next day we saw the wonder of television, in the NAAFI club, a nine inch Bush TV set with a magnifier was set up so that anyone off duty could see the coronation. I did manage to see some black dots flicker across the rain clouds above Buckingham Palace. Before returning to the section in time to see some of the same black dots become twelve Gloster Meteor Mk 8 fighters landing, in turn, on the main runway.

24

Airfield Electrician

I spent the last few months of my National Service out on the airfield, working on airfield electrical equipment. The sun always seemed to be shining and occasional low levels of work activity allowed one to sit back and watch aircraft fly.

Out at the GCA unit one could always join in a game of cricket. The only time they appeared to work was when a pilot was talked down as an exercise or the weather was bad or there had been a runway change and the whole system had to be set up again. This involved calling in a USAAF Flying Boxcar from Lakenheath. The aircraft was talked down using the system, but it did not always land.

The Boxcar was a large, twin boomed, cargo aircraft, with two enormous radial engines with four bladed propellers – about twenty-two feet in diameter – it was quite a sight to see this huge aircraft only a few feet off the deck approaching at about 200 mph, with the two yellow tipped propeller discs appearing to cut the grass.

The Royal Naval Air Service appeared on station with six Fireflies and six Sea Furies. The aircrews spent a fortnight converting from deck landings to runway landings. Both aircraft types had the same wheel (undercarriage) arrangements, two main wheels and a tail wheel mounted under the rudder.

The navy used the short runway. In the first few days of the training, aircraft would approach the runway threshold with wheels and arrester hook down, in the same attitude as if it was landing on an aircraft carrier, nearly at stalling speed. When the pilot estimated he was about thirty feet above the runway he would cut the engine. The aircraft dropped like a stone, hit the runway and bounced up well clear of concrete then it came down again. The bounces were repeated several times before the aircraft came to rest only a short distance down the runway.

The Sea Fury had a large radial engine mounted at the end of a long nose. This created a problem when the pilot taxied the aircraft. He could not see directly ahead because of the large lump in front of him. This problem was solved by the pilot standing up on the seat or swinging the aircraft to left and right to see ahead.

The pilots eventually mastered the level approach with power on and using the runway for deceleration rather than the aircraft undercarriage.

Their time on and above the airfield was an advantage when they later attacked the airfield during one of the many exercises between 'friendly' air forces.

Lex and I were servicing the flashing beacon on the far side of the airfield. Aircraft were lined up on the strip, four in the process of taking off, several more taxiing onto and off the strip, when the sound of roaring piston engines filled the air.

Two pairs of Sea Furies were flying at ground level down either side of the runway. The pair on the left turned to attack the mass of aircraft on the strip, the right hand pair were obviously attacking the aircraft taking off. The first pair turned hard to port round

Number Two hangar and disappeared, while the other two made a wider turn to port under the Meteors taking off.

The first pair came over the airfield chased by four Meteors and executed such a tight turn that they ended up flying behind the Meteors. The four Furies kept very close to the ground and finally flew off to the east and the sea chased by six Meteors.

Sometimes the squadrons had a 'wing ding'; this term had two meanings – (i) 'a massive booze up' or (ii) 'as many aircraft as possible into the air in the shortest possible time'.

I will describe the latter. Depending on service-ability, between sixty and seventy aircraft were put into the air in under ten minutes. The strip was filled with Meteors, others were parked on the taxi track by the hangars. Ground crews were given the starting order, and pilots were already in their aircraft waiting to be started in turn.

Air traffic gave the starting signal and one after another aircraft engines began to turn over, the noise increased, a heat haze developed between the rows of aircraft. Aircraft turned out of the ranks, moved off the strip and away from hangar lines. They formed a parade, two aircraft wide moving quickly along the taxi track.

Each pair turned as one onto the runway, holding the increasing engine power on the brakes until signalled to go from the red and white chequered caravan at the end of the runway. One pair became airborne as soon as possible, the next pair staying down on the runway as long as possible, and so on.

Looking from the take off end of the runway you could see aircraft continually moving down the run-way, lifting off the tarmac and rising up to join the increasing number of circling, climbing diamond formations of dark shapes in the bright sky.

On the first day, after the end of block leave 1953, Lex and I were resiting the main runway marker lamps, which had been moved off the grass onto the concrete so that the grass could be cut adjacent to the touchdown areas. We had completed the south-western end of the runway and had moved to the opposite end.

Our instructions were to clear the equipment and report to air traffic so that flying could commence. While we carried out the work aircraft were being towed out onto the apron and lined up.

The work involved setting up a pattern of sodium lamps at the end and on each side of the runway. The pattern a pilot would see as he approached the runway was a cluster of three sodiums set in the grass on the left hand side of the end of the runway. Two were at right-angles to the runway axis, the third angled at 45 degrees. On the right hand side of the runway were two more sodium lamps.

Four single sodium lamps, on each side of the runway, were set in the grass at 100 yard intervals. These lamps indicated the touchdown area.

The lamps were supplied by trailing flexible cables plugged into manholes. The clusters of lamps at the end of the runway were connected into one manhole and the cables were laid in the grass across the end of the runway. The ground beyond the runway end sloped down for about 500 yards, to an earth bank with a very dense hedge growing on it. The sandy, gravelly soil was kept ploughed up.

Lex had telephoned air traffic to say we were clear of the runway, but we still had to plug in the single sodiums. The aircraft would be taking off from the opposite end of the runway.

We had plugged in the 300 yard marker when aircraft commenced taxiing out from the apron. They took off in pairs, two getting airborne as soon as possible, the next pair staying on the runway as long as possible. This practice was to avoid the disturbed air of the previous aircraft.

We moved on to the 400 yard marker and aircraft were still taking off. Lex shouted over the engine noise that one was in trouble. The Meteor was one of a pair making the low run. When I looked up one was already airborne and the undercarriage was folding into the wings, but the other still had the main wheels in contact with the tarmac and nose wheel up.

It held this attitude for another 200 yards before the nose wheel slammed down onto the runway and masses of white to pale blue smoke poured off the main wheel tyres. The aircraft screamed past us the engine revs dropping, tyres still smoking and it eventually ran off the runway end.

It disappeared in a cloud of dust as it hit the ploughed area and the two clusters of sodium lamps followed it into the dust cloud.

We ran down to the runway end expecting to find the Meteor stuck in the ploughed up area. All we could see through the thinning dust cloud were three wheel tracks leading off to the right. At the end of the tracks were three wheels together with the remains of five sodium lamps resting against the earth bank. The hedge on top of the bank had a large gap in it. But there was still no sign of the aircraft.

We ran down to the hedge. The smell of avtag (aircraft fuel) was very strong and as we climbed onto the bank we could see the aircraft had slewed to the left and parked itself behind the hedge. A rather subdued

131

pilot officer was climbing down from the cockpit. We kept at a safe distance as we could hear the fuel gurgling out of the belly tank and the engines were still cooling down.

It was only as the pilot walked over to us that we both realised the aircraft was the one normally flown by the wing commander – flying. Its usually highly polished and pristine condition had been replaced by a dusty, slightly bent one, minus wheels and other bits and pieces.

Overheard in picture queue outside the Novere Cinema in Prince of Wales Road, Norwich when a diamond of four 74 Squadron Meteors flew overhead.

'See them jets up there Joe, armed with a seventy-five millimetre cannon, knock anything out of the sky they can'.

The speaker was referring to the in-flight refuelling probes sticking out of the noses of the Meteors.

25

Open Days

The station held several open days each year. One was
for the general public, probably to give the long
suffering population in and around Norwich an opportunity to see at close hand the aircraft which appeared
to be constantly screaming overhead and also the men
and the equipment which made it all happen. This
occasion also raised funds for the Royal Air Force
Association. Another open day was for the Royal
Observer Corps to see as many different aircraft as
possible.

The days followed a general pattern of flying
displays by individual aircraft, aerobatics by the
squadron team as well as visiting teams, static aircraft
and equipment displays. Film shows and side shows,
with refreshments provided by the NAAFI canteen.

In the days before an open day bull activities
increased. Signs and faded white lines were repainted,
new direction signs appeared – gents/ladies, no entry,
keep out – irrelevant ones dissappeared. The grass was
cut. Empty carboys outside the acc-room got returned
to stores. Odd discarded aircraft bits were removed
from the hangars. It seemed as if spring cleaning came
round more than once a year.

Visiting aircraft would start arriving a couple of days
before the show, and included several Spitfires of

various marks, one Hurricane E E Canberras, Super-marine Swifts, Hawker Hunters, North American Sabres, a Superfortress, two Whirlwind Helicopters, a Varsity, a Hastings, a Lincoln and a York, more Meteors and Vampires and many more, some with foreign markings. A Blackburn Beverley landed and stopped within 500 yards with its propellers operating in reverse.

Station flight had the job of arranging the static display and finding spaces for all the flying aircraft to be serviced. Some of the visiting aircraft brought their own ground crews with them.

The station aerobatic team always gave their flying display first. The display by four Meteors commenced with them simultaneously taking off in pairs from opposite ends of the runway followed by loops and rolls in diamond and echelon formations. One pilot would give a separate performance, while his three colleagues flew in a wide circle. They all came together to give a final loop leading into a bomb burst as they descended.

Then the other pilots, British, American, Dutch, Canadian and French all tried to go one better than the other in their flying displays. One Canberra took off on the short runway and after a very short take off run rotated and appeared to climb vertically. The next aircraft to perform was an American Sabre which took off in a similar manner but the pilot rolled the aircraft as he climbed. The Swifts and the Hunters were of great interest, the squadrons had been waiting for them for some time but none had appeared on station strength when I was demobbed.

HRH the Princess Margaret was due in Norfolk to open part of a hospital and her arrival by air, at 16.00 hours, coincided with an ROC Open Day. The brass band and the guard of honour had to be on the square at 15.30 hours in Number One dress, bulled boots, with white webbing and rifles. After an inspection by the adjutant, with the officer of the day and the station warrant officer, we were marched up to air traffic (the control tower). Here we formed into two inward-facing columns, ten feet apart and either side of the red carpet which had been laid from a waiting black Rolls Royce to the point where the aircraft was supposed to stop.

As we completed these drill movements, the flying display was stopped so that a gleaming Viking of the Queen's Flight could touch down on the main runway threshold. After taxi-ing from the far side of the airfield it finally stopped at exactly the appointed spot at 16.00 hours. Members of the ROC, male and female, pressed forward and formed a dense crowd behind each rank of the guard of honour, making sure they would see the princess in close up.

Station flight ground crew in white overalls pushed forward the steps. We were ordered to slope arms and as the Princess came out of the cabin onto the steps the order 'Royal salute present arms' was given, the band played, we were eventually commanded to slope arms and order arms as Princess Margaret descended the steps and was greeted by the AOC and the CO.

After a brief chat Princess Margaret moved down the corridor formed by the guard of honour. She was wearing a very pale green suit and a matching round hat, very attractive. She stopped to have a word with several of us, before getting into the Rolls Royce and being driven off with a police escort from the Norfolk constabulary.

Late on the following Tuesday afternoon our squadron CO cycled across from his office and called us out of the acc-room and with some more workshop staff and other passing airmen we were told to fall in on the edge of the road by Number two and Number three hangars.

We were a real scratch party and looked a sight, a right Fred Carno's army. Some of the parade were in tidy working dress, others like us were in overalls, some of them full of holes from spilt acid. We were not wearing collars, ties or berets. A car was approaching and we were ordered to 'attention' as the Rolls Royce flashed past thirty yards away doing about fifty miles an hour.

HRH probably never noticed a few of Her Majesty's faithful (but pressed) subjects bidding her farewell from RAF Horsham St Faiths.

26

Demobilisation

Demobilisation (D) day, 15 September 1953, was approaching rapidly. Eight days were left on my demob chart. A month per page calendar, with a bomber bombing out each day. My plan was to follow the practice of previous demob happy airmen, collect my 'departure' card on D-day minus five and leisurely wander round the station collecting signatures, completing it on D minus one, leaving only the SWO's office for D-day, in civilian clothes, just as I was when called up.

Chiefy knew he had lost my services when I asked him to sign my card. He said I was about number 300, of the electricians he had lost to the system and wished me good luck in the future. John and Ronnie had only been demobbed the week before.

The collection of signatures and good wishes continued up to D minus one, when I took my rifle to the armoury and dropped my bedding into the bedding store. I had arranged to kip in the pit of one of the bods who was on leave for the last night.

I also swopped items of my good (return to stores) kit with any worn out similar items with the bods in the billet. The regulars usually benefitted from this trade, but who cared.

Goodbyes were exchanged with members of the

137

electrical section and other sections. The micky was gently taken out of recently joined and still a long time to serve airmen. This was traditional, their turn to do the same would come round.

Late on the final afternoon, dressed in civvies, I packed what kit I had left together with both uniforms, issue boots and shoes, and the greatcoat into the now dirty white kitbag with the pale blue stripe and my service number, locked it up and took it down to Norwich railway station left luggage office.

My demob party was held at the Hinton Firs Pub, I stayed sober but one or two present didn't. The next morning, after breakfast, complete with attaché case and my nearly completed departure card I walked into station headquarters and into the station warrant officer's office. A clerk took my card, checked it and after a while searched for and found my discharge papers and travel warrant. He then asked for my form 1250 – RAF identification card – which he took and asked me to wait. The clerk left the office with my papers, when he came back he said, follow me, and led me into the station adjutant's office.

The adjutant asked me to sit down and for few moments discussed my two years in the Royal Air Force. He closed the conversation by asking 'If I had considered signing on as a regular.' My reply was 'yes and no'. Yes I had considered and no I would not be signing on.

On receipt of the standard answer the Adjutant then thanked me for my time spent in the service and gave me his best wishes for the future. I reciprocated. He gave me my discharge papers and I left the office and headquarters, crossed the road to the guardroom, showed my papers to the snoop on duty, and was once more wished 'Good luck, you lucky sod'. The snoop was obviously a National Service Airman, and I walked out of the gates of RAF Horsham St Faiths for the last time.

Retrospect

I had decided at the outset that I would enjoy my period of National Service as far as it was possible to do so.

There were periods of despair. Such times were usually associated with the attitudes of those who were trying to train us. They had only one method, the whip. I don't think they had heard about the carrot. Also they were responding to having to train material which at the first opportunity would attempt to thwart their – sometimes – ridiculous objectives.

But, generally speaking, once on permanant posting life was pleasant and comfortable, apart from the need to still bull your kit, clean the billet and take part in the ceremonial bull every week.

It was also a happy time if you set out to enjoy it. Some National Service airmen hated every second of their service and they regularly voiced their prejudice. The enclosed and secure life on the station – all found – tended to isolate one from the outside world, even though the centre of Norwich was only a bus ride away.

Finally, two years was too long. The second year was spent repeating what had happened in the previous six months. Most National Service RAF tradesmen had reached the rank of SAC or JT by the end of the first year and any further progress was barred because one was not a regular airman. The Royal Air Force's only carrot to further promotion was 'sign on'.

The immediate postwar period and well into the sixties was a time of full employment, probably made possible by continuously keeping about half a million of Britain's young men out of normal employment in National Service, to serve and also to die in Egypt, Palestine, Malaya, Korea, Cyprus, Aden, Central Europe and the United Kingdom.

APPENDIX

Airforce Lingo – Slang

Acc
— an accumulator – a rechargeable electric cell or a battery.

Air Traffic
— the control tower – it controlled air traffic.

AOC –
Air Officer Commanding.

Barrack damages
— cash assessment payable for damaged billet fixtures and fittings.

Billet
— building or hut used as living accommodation.

Biscuits
— mattress made up of three separate equal squares.

Blanco
— paste polish for cleaning/decorating webbing etc. Available in many colours.

Bod
— a person.

Box
— aircraft, added to shortened aircraft name. e.g. – Meteor becomes metbox, pronounced meatbox. Possibly from the Wright Brothers' Boxkite, aircrew used the expression 'kite'.

Brasso
— trade name for a liquid metal polish.

Bull
— a tall story, or excessive and unnecessary cleaning.

141

Bull night	– an evening spent cleaning inside and outside the billet, the corridors and associated ablution facilities, as well as one's uniforms and boots etc. Usually the night before the weekly inspection.
Bumph	– toilet paper or any official paperwork, referred to as a load of 'bumph'.
Button stick	– item of kit, brass plate about six inches long, with a slot and indentations cut into it, to allow buttons, badges and buckles to be cleaned, without getting metal polish on the fabric.
Char	– tea.
Chocks	– common expression for any wedge-shaped device placed under or against round objects to stop them moving. An RAF wheel chock consisted of two hinged aluminium plates with a chain attached to them. When pulled the chain collapsed the plates allowing the chock to be dragged away from the wheel.
CO or OC	– Commanding Officer or Officer Commanding.
Detachment	– temporary posting away from permanent unit, usually to attend courses or temporarily reinforce staff at another station.
Erk	– an airman, AC 1 or AC 2 – the lowest of the low.
Frog	– separate piece of webbing slipped

	onto waist webbing belt to hold bayonet scabbard.
Fizzer	– a charge. RAF form 252 was the charge sheet, the record of some misdemeanour and was the start of formal disciplinary action against the accused.
GCA	– ground controlled approach, radar assisted talk down aircraft landing system.
H block	– (aitch block) – permanent billet block, usually on two floors, the billets forming the sides of the H and the ablution facility connecting the two sides across the middle.
Housewife	– (Hussif) item of kit, containing needles, cotton, wool, spare buttons etc., to darn your socks, sew on a button or rank badges.
Jankers	– on station punishment, following a fizzer, loss of privileges.
Irons	– short for eating irons, viz knife, fork and spoon.
Last three	– the last three numbers of one's service number, i.e. No. 1234567 – 567 is the last three.
Leave	– time off station or holiday.
KD	– khaki drill, material used for over-alls etc.
Kip	– to sleep.
Kiwi	– tradename for one make of boot polish.
Mess	– building housing kitchens and feeding facilities.
Naafi	– the Navy, Army and Air Force

	Institutes. Recreation clubs with canteen facilities.
Nissen hut	– semi-circular shaped hut of corrugated iron sheets, named after inventor – P.N. Nissen.
Pass	– document allowing a bod to be off station.
Pit	– a bed.
Posted	– ordered to move to another unit.
Posting	– appointed RAF abode, home or abroad, training or service unit.
Rank	– (i) drill – each flight is formed of three ranks, front rank, middle rank and rear rank.
Rank	– (ii) title, e.g. Squadron Leader, Sergeant etc.
Snowdrop/Snoop	–a member of the RAF Police, derived from the white peaked hat worn by the police and their snooping activities.
Spider	– grouping of six or eight huts and an ablution block to form a spider shape. The huts represent the legs and the ablution block the body.
Sprog	– brand new airman, completely untrained.
Square	– parade ground, an area of tarmac or concrete, not necessarily square, used for cermonial parades, inspections etc. Square bashing – time spent on parade ground performing drill movements. Derived from the need to stamp one's boots on the ground to create maximum sound, e.g. to bash the square.

SWO	– Station Warrant Officer.
Tannoy	– public address system of loud-speakers fixed in all buildings and on poles and walls in open spaces on all RAF stations. Tannoy is the name of the maker.
Travel warrant	– document exchanged for bus or train ticket for travel between named points.
U/S	– unserviceable, faulty, not fit for use, Naff.
WAAF	– Women's Auxiliary Air Force, later WRAF – Auxiliary became Royal.
Wads	– sandwiches.
Webbing	– tightly woven cotton fabric, used for belts, haversacks, slings and straps.
Wing Ding	– a large organised booze up or several squadrons of aircraft airborne at the same time in one formation.

This list is only a small example of the RAF jargon.